365 DAYS IN THE Psalms

WORDS FOR LIFE

BroadStreet
PUBLISHING

BroadStreet Publishing Group, LLC.
Savage, Minnesota, USA
Broadstreetpublishing.com

365 Days in the *Psalms*

© 2023 by BroadStreet Publishing®

9781424566358

Devotional entries composed by Janelle Anthony Breckell.

Typesetting and design by Garborg Design Works | garborgdesign.com
Editorial services by Michelle Winger | literallyprecise.com

Printed in China.

23 24 25 26 27 28 29 7 6 5 4 3 2 1

Give thanks
to the LORD,
for he is good!
His faithful love
endures forever.

Psalm 136:1 NLT

*J*ust as the psalmist encountered, we can be overwhelmed by the circumstances of life. We run into situations that are frustrating and discouraging. But we also experience the peace and protection of our wonderful Creator whose goodness is not dependent on our situation.

Depression and anxiety may threaten to steal our hope and joy, but the psalms are full of God's unchanging love and faithfulness. As we offer our prayers and praise to God, we can also choose to believe that each day will be filled with his perfect promises.

Find the hope, joy, and peace that is abundant in God as you reflect on these devotional entries, psalms, and prayers.

January

*May he grant your heart's desires
and make all your plans succeed.*

PSALM 20:4 NLT

Book of Life

Your eyes beheld my unformed substance.
In your book were written
all the days that were formed for me,
when none of them as yet existed.
PSALM 139:16 NRSV

It's the day of new beginnings and you might be feeling a mixture of emotions. There is bound to be excitement about the possibilities that are waiting just around the corner, but there also might be overwhelming thoughts about the trials that could lie ahead or fear of the unknown.

Whatever your thoughts and feelings are about this day, remember that you have the spirit of Christ in your heart and mind, ready to help you in all of your decisions and strengthening you through any challenges. Head into this day with the confidence that he created you and already knows who you are, and who you are going to become!

Lord, thank you that you know me better than I know myself because you created me. Give me courage to take on this year with grace and skill, knowing that you are right with me.

Family History

I will sing of the steadfast love of the Lord, forever;
with my mouth I will make known your faithfulness
to all generations.
PSALM 89:1 NIV

If you think back through your family history, where did the message of Jesus start? You might have a long history of believers, or you might be the first one of your family to believe. Either way, God allows his message to transfer throughout the generations.

Thank the Lord that you have either been a part of a long heritage of faith, or that you are the very first fresh beginning of a faith that will go beyond you. Sing of the love of your Lord!

God, I am so thankful that the story of your steadfast love is passed on through generations. Help me to remember that I am a significant part of passing on this truth.

Blessed with Peace

The LORD gives strength to his people;
the LORD blesses his people with peace.
PSALM 29:11 NIV

What are the most relaxed times of your day or week? Is it when you go for a walk, or sit on the porch in the evening? It could be that first waking moment of your day when everything is quiet and calm. Peace is a very big part of the story of relaxing, whether it is having a calm spirit, a still body, or a still mind. We crave those moments in our ever increasingly busy world.

Before you approach the busy times, ask the Lord for peace. The psalm here says that he gives strength and blesses with peace. Rely on that promise, drink it in, until you feel equipped for the day ahead.

Lord, thank you that I have this moment right now to still my heart, mind, and body. I accept the blessing of peace that you have promised.

Pushed Back

I was pushed back and about to fall,
but the LORD helped me.
PSALM 118:13 NIV

When you watch the way wild animals behave when they are trapping their prey, one of the main strategies is to corner their prey so there is nowhere to escape. The picture in this verse is like this except the corner looks more like a cliff's edge!

Have there been times in your life when you felt like you were up against a wall, either with the pressure of other people, or with something that you got yourself into? You may have felt like there was no relief or escape. These are the times when you need your great rescuer to show up on and help you in your troubles. God will not allow you to fall.

Lord, thank you for rescuing me every time I have felt backed into a corner. Thank you that you come to my aid in my times of distress.

This Is the Day

This is the day the LORD has made.
We will rejoice and be glad in it.
PSALM 118:24 NLT

When winter is fully upon us, it is not as warm outside, and there's not as much life in nature. If you live where winter is cold, you may be growing tired of boots, hats, scarves (well, maybe not scarves), and puffy, shapeless coats. Looking outside, there may not be much to feel particularly joyful about.

The simple truth is that God made today, and he made it with you in it. As you go into your day today, either with excitement or dread, encourage yourself that this is a day purposed by the Lord, for you. Make the most out of it!

Lord, I wasn't that happy to get out of bed this morning, but now that I am up, I commit this day to you and thank you for making it.

From Birth

From birth I have relied on you;
you brought me forth from my mother's womb.
I will ever praise you.
PSALM 71:6 NIV

Although mothers have to go through an incredible process to birth a child, they are not ultimately responsible for the first breath of that child. This is a gift from God—from our development in the womb, to our first breath, to our growth.

We rely on our Creator and his perfect design. It's something worth recognizing and praising him for. Your life is from him, and through him. Rejoice in this beautiful gift today.

Creator God, thank you for the beauty of the created human form. Thank you that I am a part of this beautiful creation. I choose to praise you for creating me just as I am.

Troubled Thoughts

Listen to my prayer, O God, do not ignore my plea;
hear me and answer me.
My thoughts trouble me and I am distraught.
PSALM 55:1-2 NIV

Life is not always joyful. Often we search the Scriptures for comfort, assurance, and hope, and we will certainly find those things there. But we will also find words like the ones here. Ones that immediately feel like we had written them ourselves.

In times of pain and distress, particularly emotional and mental stress, it's amazing how much it helps to know that we are not alone. It has been a part of the human condition to sometimes feel ignored by God and to feel troubled and distraught. But you are not alone. Take comfort in that today.

Lord, on those mornings when I wake up and feel troubled, help me to remember that I am not alone. You are always with me.

Crushed

The LORD is close to the brokenhearted;
he rescues those whose spirits are crushed.
PSALM 34:18 NLT

What are the things that break your heart? Thoughts of people in poverty, your own child struggling with friends, a parent who has suddenly passed away? Life is full of heartache. The greater the love, the greater the loss. We hurt because we love. We can find some courage in that thought as we navigate difficult emotions.

To be able to love is an amazing gift, and life wouldn't be so full if we didn't have love. Enjoy the love you have and try to find a way to appreciate loss because it tells you how fully you are able to love.

Lord, thank you for giving me a heart that is capable of loving others. Please rescue my crushed spirit when I am in the middle of heartache. Be my comfort and my strength.

Lit Up

Your word is a lamp to my feet,
and a light to my path.
PSALM 119:105 NKJV

Walking around in the dark is no fun. You can trip over things, be frightened by shadows, and feel lost. As soon as you have any amount of light, your assurance comes back. You can see the space in front of your feet and the path directly ahead. You can move your source of light around to find out what those lurking shadows are.

Everything is better with the light, and this Scripture says the best way to have light in our lives is to know God's Word. Take some time to soak yourself in his Word and let it be a light for your path today.

Lord, reveal the truth of your Word to me today. Guide me as I step into each choice that I make along the way.

Hear Me

Hear me when I call, O God of my righteousness!
You have relieved me in my distress;
Have mercy on me, and hear my prayer.
PSALM 4:1 NKJV

Who do you call when you are feeling upset and stressed? Is there someone in your life who you know will listen to you in your time of need?

It is a good feeling when someone really listens to you. Are you confident that God is always near and ready for you to call on him when you are distressed? Call out to him when you are troubled and wait for his mercy.

Hear me when I call, O God of my righteousness! You have relieved me when I have been troubled and stressed with circumstances in my life. Have mercy on me and hear my prayer.

Considering Grief

You, God, see the trouble of the afflicted;
you consider their grief and take it in hand.
The victims commit themselves to you;
you are the helper of the fatherless.
PSALM 10:14 NIV

The problems of life are seen all around us sometimes on a daily basis. We see troubled families, poverty, and sickness. Maybe you are experiencing some of these afflictions now. It is comforting to know that God sees all of your trouble.

God doesn't stand at a distance. This Scripture says that he takes your grief in his hand. Take his hand today. He is your good father who cares so much for you.

Lord, help me trust you as a good father who is always there to help me in my time of need.

Boundaries

Happy are those whom you discipline, O Lord,
and whom you teach out of your law.
PSALM 94:12 NRSV

Discipline of a child is often followed by tears, so it seems surprising when the Bible associates discipline with happiness. While we may feel ashamed when the Lord convicts our heart of wrongdoing, we need to recognize that God's correction is ultimately for our good.

God wants us to do what is right because he loves us. When we remember that he loves us, it takes the sting out of discipline and helps us to choose what is right.

Lord, thank you for guiding me into every good thing. Give me ears to hear and eyes to see the truth of your ways. Help me to learn from your instruction and to know your grace when I need correction. Let me experience the joy of your discipline.

Sing to the King

Sing praises to God, sing praises!
Sing praises to our King, sing praises!
PSALM 47:6 NKJV

We may not all have the voice of an angel, but we can all sing—no matter how good or bad it sounds to us. God created us each with a voice and with lips that can praise him for all the good things he has done.

God is the King of the earth and the King of our hearts. He will delight in our songs of praise even if he is the only one that appreciates them. We should sing praises to God because we understand his goodness and his grace. We should sing because he is worthy.

God, you are the King of all the earth. You have been good to me. You have shown your grace toward me. Teach me to delight in singing your praises. I know you delight in me when I praise you.

Open Eyes

The LORD opens the eyes of those who are blind;
The LORD raises up those who are bowed down;
The Lord loves the righteous.

PSALM 146:8 NASB

Our God loves to restore life to his creation. When Jesus came to earth, he healed many physical needs, restoring people to health. But greater than physical healing, Jesus came to restore our spiritual brokenness. He opened eyes to the truth, ministered to the poor in spirit, and restored believers to righteousness.

Have you experienced healing from your brokenness? If you are feeling broken right now, bring it to the gentle healer and know that he will restore you to fullness.

God, I am feeling a little fragile right now. I have felt broken, disappointed, and discouraged, but I trust in your faithfulness. I believe that you are in the process of restoring me.

Mad

Be angry, and do not sin.
Meditate within your heart on your bed,
and be still.
PSALM 4:4 NKJV

Have you ever been mad enough to notice that you are trembling? Sometimes we can get overwhelmed with emotions of anger, sometimes for good reasons and other times not. Whatever the reason, the Bible speaks of the need to take some time out to calm down.

God is not overly concerned with the fact that we get angry. He understands the emotions of his creation, but acting out in anger has never achieved anything good. Be aware of your temper today and find a place to be still if it all gets to be too much.

Father, help me to stay in control of myself even when I am irritated or upset with someone. Give me good strategies for getting out of sin's way.

Complaints

I pour out my complaint before Him;
I declare before Him my trouble.
PSALM 142:2 NKJV

Life's not fair. Think of games, or races, or even schooling. Someone always comes out on top, and there are always losers. We can influence some outcomes, but there are many things that are outside of our control.

We cannot guarantee that we will be protected from the troubles of this life. What do we do when we feel like complaining about our misfortunes? We often feel like we have no right to complain to God—we are told to be thankful in all things, right? Well, God can handle your complaints and your cry for answers. Remember how David cried out to him in the Psalms.

Lord, I'm glad that you can handle my complaints and my honest heart. I know that this is the safest place to vent my frustrations because only you can help me to change my heart from grumpiness to gratitude.

Steady Steps

The LORD makes firm the steps of the one who delights in him.
PSALM 37:23 NIV

If you've ever taken the hand of a toddler, you'll know that they are relying on you for their balance. If they stumble, you can easily steady them. This simple act of holding a hand means that you and the child have confidence that they won't fall flat on their face.

In the same way, when we commit our way to the Lord, we are essentially placing our hand in his. He delights in the fact that we are walking with him and even in the times when we stumble, he will steady our path and give us the confidence to keep walking.

Jesus, I invite you to take my hand and stand beside me today. Keep my steps firm and keep me from falling.

Nothing Expected

*What can I ever give back to God
to repay him for the blessings he's poured out on me?*
PSALM 116:12 TPT

One of the gifts the Lord has given us is the gift of grace. He expects nothing from us when he has given us everything. We wrestle, like the writer of this psalm, with how to repay God for the gift of unconditional love.

God does not ask for repayment; he desires devotion. Follow him. Pursue him. He desires a relationship with you above all else and that is attainable if you allow him in. You will find that being devoted to him is the best gift you can give yourself.

God, I know you don't expect repayment but I desire to walk in step with you as I go through my day. You have given me so much and I know you want my heart. Help me give that to you today.

Celebrations

They celebrate your abundant goodness
and joyfully sing of your righteousness.
PSALM 145:7 NIV

There are some church services and Christian celebrations that are so full of the Holy Spirit it's beautifully overwhelming. Have you experienced that? In a remarkable way, believers come together to celebrate all that God has done in their lives. Some dance, sing at the top of their lungs, or cry tears of joy. How happy that sight must make our Father in heaven!

Can you find a worship song and joyfully sing out to the God who loves you today? He does not care what you sound like; it is music to his ears. God adores you and cherishes you. He is proud to call you his child. What a good, good Father!

Father, thank you for loving me with a perfect love. Today I want to spend time praising you in song. I thank you for the gift of your goodness and love. I am forever thankful for the ways you love me.

All Good

You are good, and what you do is good;
teach me your decrees.
PSALM 119:68 NIV

Wherever you are in your life, it is possible to feel the goodness of the God who loves you. Even if you can't see the story he has written for you unfolding in the way you'd like, you need to believe that he is still good. His mysteries that are intertwined in your story are not always yours to know. Just trust in his goodness.

Teaching yourself to claim victory over sin and speak truth over lies takes practice, patience, and a lot of prayer. Use the Word of God to gain understanding. Reading Scripture every day will equip you with the tools you need and give you armor to take each curve in your story with more ease and trust.

Jesus, remind me that you are living and active. Your Word is truth; let me use it to train my thoughts. I praise you for your goodness. Thank you for loving me.

Tender Mercies

LORD, don't hold back your tender mercies from me.
Let your unfailing love and faithfulness always protect me.
PSALM 40:11 NLT

Often we think of protection as a guard against things that we don't want to happen. We pray for protection from illness, from tragedy, and from hardship. Yet there might be a different story written for our lives that may not be void of tragedy.

In the circle of life and sin of man, it is inevitable that life will be hard at times. In the same breath, God's tender mercies come to us. He does not hide them. He does not take them away. We serve a God who is tender and loving. His mercies are new every morning.

God, thank you that you are a tender, loving father. You know me better than I know myself. May I always see you as my protector and may I feel your mercy no matter where I am.

Feathers and Wings

His massive arms are wrapped around you, protecting you.
You can run under his covering of majesty and hide.
His arms of faithfulness are a shield keeping you from harm.
PSALM 91:4 TPT

We want to run and hide from many things in life, thinking that if we can run, difficulty will surely be gone when we choose to come back. We run because of fear. We run because of anger. We run because of indifference. We run, hoping someone will chase us. Hoping someone will come and find us.

God knows. He knows you. You matter to him. You mean something to the Creator of your life. He is not beyond whatever you are facing today. He tells you to run to him and he promises shelter and protection. He promises you that he will meet you in that place and give you peace. Run to him.

What a faithful father you are, God! I'm grateful to you for your love, protection, and shelter from all the things of this world that scare me. With you, I am safe. With you, I know I am loved no matter what I'm facing.

Mercy Seat

You, O Lord, your mercy-seat love is limitless,
reaching higher than the highest heavens.
Your great faithfulness is so infinite,
stretching over the whole earth.

PSALM 36:5 TPT

The world is a huge place; yet we often feel we are the only ones suffering. Our circumstances can stretch before us like a mountain, insurmountable to conquer. But God is not contained. He does not have boundaries.

In his Word, God says that even faith as small as a mustard seed can move mountains (Matthew 17:20). The God we serve is passionate about the pursuit of his people and his faithfulness is forever.

To know that your love spans the entire earth, God, is a powerful reminder to me of your sovereignty. Let me trust in your faithfulness as I face my day today. Thank you for your love and mercy.

Heart of Integrity

He shepherded them according to the integrity of his heart,
And guided them with his skillful hands.
PSALM 78:72 NASB

How humbling it must have been for David to be called by God to do something great: to lead an entire nation! Psalms tell us that God presented David as the one to love and care for them with integrity and a pure heart.

Think of people in your life who display integrity, who seem pure of heart. They are the people others look to for guidance. Think about what it means to shepherd with integrity and make that your mission with whomever you are given the opportunity to lead.

God, help me to use the gifting you gave me for the greater good of your kingdom. I want to work on the areas of sin in my life, always bringing them to the cross. Thank you for creating me uniquely. Help me to find purpose in each day.

With Passion

Listen to me all you godly ones: Love the Lord with passion!
The Lord protects and preserves all those who are loyal to him.
But he pays back in full all those who reject him in their pride.
PSALM 31:23 TPT

We put our heart and soul into the people, jobs, or hobbies that we are most excited about—the ones we love the most. They fuel us in a way that gives us energy. They motivate and inspire us to be our best. These passions can be our report card, giving us praise or critique depending on how we're doing.

It is with this very same passion that we should love, praise, and serve the Lord! Our greatest efforts should go toward our relationship with Jesus, the one who freed us from our bondage, and deeply pursues our heart.

Jesus, I want to put my effort toward my relationship with you. You deserve all my praise, my time, and my energy. I am my best self when I am in relationship with you. Guide my passion by your Spirit.

Bubbling Over

We laughed and laughed, and overflowed with gladness.
We were left shouting for joy and singing your praise.
All the nations saw it and joined in, saying,
"The Lord has done great miracles for them!"
PSALM 126:2 TPT

Laughter is one of the greatest sounds in the world. An old married couple dancing. A toddler being tickled. A pair of best friends sharing a joke. When you hear laughter, you can't help but crack a smile yourself.

Imagine what God must feel when he hears his children laughing, singing, and praising him together. Imagine what happiness must sound like to him. Picture a room full of believers singing in harmony to show their love for him. What a joyous, beautiful sound that must be!

Jesus, I love you and I worship your name. I want to start my day in praise for you. Hear my voice and let it be pleasing to you.

Glistening like Gold

The daughters of kings, women of honor, are maidens in your courts.
And standing beside you, glistening in your pure and golden glory,
is the beautiful bride-to-be!
PSALM 45:9 TPT

One of the best parts of a wedding is when the bride is about to walk down the aisle. She is beautiful in her gown. On her arm is someone she loves, usually her dad or a father figure, giving her away.

Most of the time, all eyes are on the bride. But have you ever looked at the groom in that moment? At the end of the aisle is a groom, waiting for his life to start with a woman he adores. Beholding that look is equally precious! In this psalm we are reminded that Jesus is waiting for us at the altar. What a beautiful picture this is.

Jesus, I am glad you are waiting for me. I gladly take your arm and choose to walk in dignity and honor throughout my life.

Pass It On

God, let your goodness be given away to your good people,
to all your godly lovers!
PSALM 125:4 TPT

God does not have a reserve tank of goodness that dries up. His goodness cannot and does not end. Let that truth settle for a minute. We live in a world where we can't always see God's goodness. We turn on the news and see people harming each other. We do life with people who have destructive behaviors. We know someone with cancer, or someone who has lost a child.

We may have experienced some of these difficult things for ourselves. We have a lot of questions and not always a lot of answers, but we can lean into Christ for our answers today. He is good no matter how we feel in any particular moment.

Jesus Christ, I know that you came to save this world and make it whole again. Help me to see goodness even in the middle of the muck of this world.

Kindness

From your kindness you send the rain to water the mountains
from the upper rooms of your palace.
Your goodness brings forth fruit for all to enjoy.
PSALM 104:13 TPT

You know the concept of paying it forward? You do a kind act for someone, and, in turn, they pass that kindness on to another person, and so it continues. Kind act after kind act spreads goodness and service to people all over.

This is fruit of the Spirit as described in the Bible. What we do here, in the name of God, will produce lasting effects. Do something kind today, or maybe gratefully accept someone else's kindness.

God, I am blessed by the kindness that you freely shower on me. You take care of all your creation. Let me be at peace today because I know you are taking care of me.

Shadowed

Because you are my helper,
I sing for joy in the shadow of your wings.
PSALM 63:7 NLT

God is our greatest cheerleader. He watches as we take flight in a calling he has put before us, and he gently encourages us, urging us forward and cheering us on.

The God of the universe, the Creator of everything, the one living on the throne of righteousness, knows us and cheers us on. What a privilege and an honor to know that once he sets us down a path, he will not let us stray without first urging us forward for his mission.

Father God, thank you that you help me in times of trouble and times of joy. Thank you that I walk safely in the shadow of your wings every day, and that you are my shield and protector.

Never Ending

*You are the Lord who reigns over your never-ending kingdom
through all the ages of time and eternity!
You are faithful to fulfill every promise you've made.
You manifest yourself as kindness in all you do!*

PSALM 145:13 TPT

God's kingdom never ends. The faithful men and women we read about in the Bible are with God in eternity. The people we do life with now all have an eternal fate. The kids and grandkids and descendants of ours that haven't yet been born will live on this earth until Jesus comes back.

As you head into your day, think about who has been before you and who will be after you. God's promise goes on and on!

I am so glad to be a part of your kingdom, Lord! Help me to live as a child of eternity assured that you are in my past, present, and future.

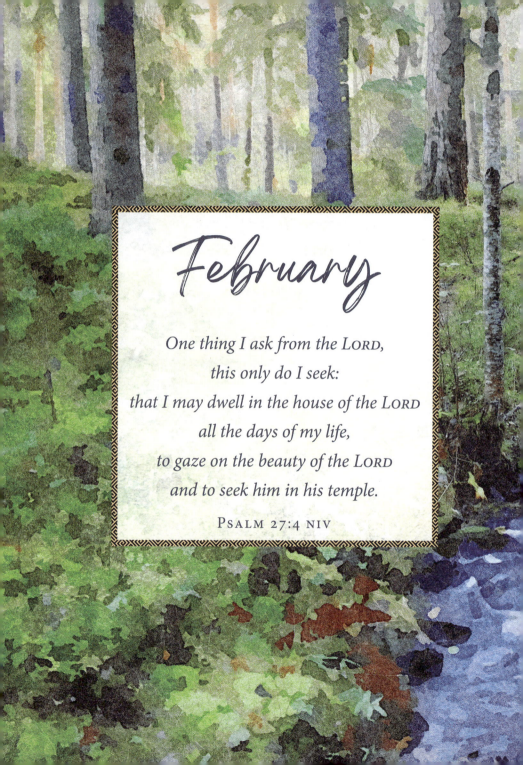

February

One thing I ask from the Lord,
this only do I seek:
that I may dwell in the house of the Lord
all the days of my life,
to gaze on the beauty of the Lord
and to seek him in his temple.

PSALM 27:4 NIV

A Forever Song

This forever-song I sing of the gentle love of God!
Young and old alike will hear about your faithful,
steadfast love—never failing!
PSALM 89:1 TPT

Have you ever turned on the radio and heard a song that instantly brought you back to a particular memory? Clear as day, you can feel the same emotions, picture exactly where you were when you heard it and immediately feel as young as you did in the times you sang it out loud.

Music is a beautiful way for us to create a soundtrack of life, piecing together songs for the years we heard them. Enjoy God's gift of music today.

Holy Spirit, put songs in my heart today that bring me joy and comfort. I want to be overwhelmed with your presence!

Be Brave

In God, whose word I praise—
in God I trust and am not afraid.
What can mere mortals do to me?
PSALM 56:4 NIV

"In God We Trust." This is still printed on US currency despite many people not truly having trust, or even a belief in God. As Christians, we claim to trust God.

Is this a motto that is written on the currency of your heart, one that you can hold fast to in times when all else seems to be against you? You might spend some money today. If you do, remind yourself of your trust in God as you hand over your cash.

God, I do truly trust in you. There are times when I don't hear you and when I'm not sure of what you are leading me toward. But I choose to trust because you are a God who keeps your word.

Wherever I Go

If I fly with wings into the shining dawn, you're there!
If I fly into the radiant sunset, you're there waiting.
PSALM 139:9 TPT

Moving on from anywhere can be disconcerting. A new circumstance, house, or even country means that we have to leave what we have been comfortable with and step out into the unknown.

Take courage that no matter where you go, the Lord will always go with you. He is as far east as the rising sun, and as far west as the sunset. He will guide you as you move, and he will hold you when you get there.

Lord, this world is small in comparison to your presence. You promise to be with me wherever I go. Guide me in the next step of my life; give me confidence to move on to where you have called me. I trust in you from the rising of the sun to its going down.

Don't Forget

My whole being, praise the Lord
and do not forget all his kindnesses.
PSALM 103:2 NCV

Did you wake up with aches and pains or feeling a little out of sorts? Our God is a God of restoration. He shows us his kindness, through his love, in that he cares for our entire being.

Not only does God want to restore a right relationship with you, he also wants to restore your body to health. Be kind to your body today, and ask God to restore whatever part of your being doesn't feel quite right.

Thank you, Jesus, for the gift of life. Thank you for this body, this vessel that you use to give expression to my heart and soul. Help me to take care of this beautiful being.

Home

Surely goodness and mercy shall follow me all the days of my life;
and I will dwell in the house of the LORD forever.
PSALM 23:6 NKJV

We leave footprints as we walk along this journey of life. Some of these footprints are left from walking in the dirt and they need to be cleaned up because they don't belong to the path of righteousness.

God wants to lead you in the right direction. As you live in his ways, your path will be followed by goodness, and his mercy will clean up those footsteps that have gone in the wrong direction. His grace will follow you all your life and it is by this grace that you will dwell in the house of the Lord forever.

Heavenly Father, I want to dwell in your house forever. I trust in your goodness and mercy to follow me as I journey this life with you before me, behind me, and beside me. Allow me to know your presence today.

Nothing Beside You

Whom have I in heaven but you?
And earth has nothing I desire besides you.
PSALM 73:25 NIV

When God said, "I am," he declared how all-encompassing his presence is both in heaven and on earth. When we begin to understand the love and the greatness of our God, we become convinced that he is everything.

The Lord is your all; there is nothing in heaven and earth that is greater, and his love for you will give you everything you need. While everything else around you may fail and fall away, the knowledge of God will forever rest in your heart. He is your portion forever.

Holy God, you are the reason for all life, for my life, and for eternal life. Thank you that your love is enough to sustain my heart. My body may fail me, and my words may never be able to express my gratefulness to you, but you are more than enough for me both in this life and the life to come.

Light Dawns

Even in darkness light dawns for the upright,
for those who are gracious and compassionate and righteous.
PSALM 112:4 NIV

The middle of the night can be an anxious time to be awake, often bringing irrational fears of danger, disturbing thoughts, or a disquieted spirit. In contrast, the first rays of light in the morning can bring peace, hope, and joy.

Life does not always seem full of hope and joy especially when you have experienced hurt, anxiety, or depression. God's truth is that even in your moments of darkness his light will dawn for you. Grace, compassion, and righteousness belong to you as you allow Jesus to shine his life into your heart.

Jesus, sometimes I despair over the darkness in this world. In these times, I choose to trust in the light that you bring into my life and into the world. Let me experience the hope and joy that comes with the dawn.

Many Wonders

Many, O LORD my God, are the wonders you have done.
The things you planned for us no one can recount to you;
were I to speak and tell of them,
they would be too many to declare.
PSALM 40:5 NIV

It is good to give God the glory for all the things that we find too wonderful for words. We know from the Bible that God has acted powerfully on many occasions to preserve his chosen people. We know that Jesus performed spectacular miracles. The Holy Spirit moved mightily on the early church and still shows his power to us today.

Remember today the many wonders God has done in your life and in the lives of others around you. Thank him for the interest he has shown in you and for the constant revelation of his goodness and love.

Holy Spirit, I believe in your power, and yet sometimes I forget to rely on you! Help me to use the strength that I have found through you to get through each day. Your wonders are too many to declare.

Search Me

Search me, God, and know my heart;
Put me to the test and know my anxious thoughts;
And see if there is any hurtful way in me,
And lead me in the everlasting way.
PSALM 139:23-24 NASB

Searching requires looking in every place available to see what is there. Asking God to search your heart means that you are inviting him to know everything that is in it. Vulnerability is hard particularly when we are battling pride or when we want to hide painful feelings or even sin.

Try to be a little more comfortable with vulnerability before God today. Right now, it's just you and him. Tell him exactly how you feel and let him show you how he feels. There is nothing better than hearing how much he loves you.

Lord, I'm so glad that you know me so well. Not only did you create me, but you have been with me every step of the way, so you understand my past, present, and my future.

Please Answer

Turn and answer me, O LORD my God!
Restore the sparkle to my eyes, or I will die.
PSALM 13:3 NLT

There's an age old saying that the eyes are the window to the soul. You can probably describe those times when you looked in someone's eyes and saw sadness, pain, or regret. Equally, eyes show joy and contentment—what we might refer to as a sparkle.

Going through tough times can take that sparkle away. When you lose hope, joy, or peace, your eyes will tell the story. You may feel that in this moment your joy has slipped away from you. Ask the Lord to turn and answer you. Ask him for hope. Ask him to restore that spark of life so you might live life fully.

Lord, as I stare down the path of another day, I pray I would see goodness, and hope, and light. Save me from despair with the hope of your presence with me.

Preserved with Integrity

Let integrity and uprightness protect me,
For I wait for You.
PSALM 25:21 NASB

When you think of great leaders who have stood the test of time, what is it that really defines them? A good leader has integrity. They can withstand all kinds of difficulties because in the midst of them they are preserved by the very fact that they cannot be faulted by immorality or injustice. We might not like some of the characteristics or personality traits of certain leaders, but if they have proven time and time again to be people of their word, they will continue to flourish.

This Scripture attests to the principle that being a person of integrity will preserve your life and keep you from all kinds of accusations. If you are tempted to stray today, remember to wait for the Lord to rescue you.

Lord, thank you for the people in my life who have modeled integrity. Keep them strong and preserved for your glory. Help me to be a leader who is fully of integrity too.

The Trap

Keep me free from the trap that is set for me,
for you are my refuge.
PSALM 31:4 NIV

Have you ever had to set up a trap for a pest that you didn't want in or around your house? Perhaps it was just a tiny mouse, but you set up the bait and left it overnight so the pesky little thing would think it was safe in the dark, still house while it searched around for the prize of a piece of cheese.

You may have seen traps set in the woods that trigger a whole net to fall on an unsuspecting animal when a rock or stick is moved. There is always a lure or something that encourages that animal to head to the trap. Life is full of traps and we have to choose wisdom every step of the way. Ask for God to give you discernment to know what to avoid.

Lord, I need your help as I discern what traps might be set before me. I know I can't live in fear of what might happen, so I choose to live in your refuge.

Signs

Show me a sign of your favor,
that those who hate me may see and be put to shame
because you, LORD, have helped me and comforted me.
PSALM 86:17 ESV

As you drive today, take note of the signs that you see along the way. There are all kinds of road signs: some that tell you to stop, give way, move over, or slow down. There are signs that tell you road works are approaching, or to watch out for deer or other animals in the area. Signs give us a signal of what is coming up and guide us in the right direction.

In the same way, God can give us signs to lead us to the right things. This is how he shows favor. It is not just by showering us with blessing, it is by showing us the right way. When we walk in righteousness, we will be blessed.

Lord, thank you for guiding me with your signs and keeping me going in the right direction. Help me to see your signs and pay attention today.

I Love You

I love you, LORD, my strength.
PSALM 18:1 NIV

It is three simple words, yet they can hold such power, beauty, and hope. God is love and we will never stop learning about what this means to us. Today, however, think of your love for God and what he means to you. There are so many reasons why we love God, but perhaps you could just simply express those three words to him and let your adoration for him be enough.

On this day when you are reminded of people's love for each other, don't forget to acknowledge the one who is defined in his very nature as love, and offer this love unconditionally to you. Dwell in his love.

I love you, Lord, my strength.

Light Care

Send me your light and your faithful care,
let them lead me;
let them bring me to your holy mountain,
to the place where you dwell.

PSALM 43:3 NIV

In the time of Old Testament Israel, God's presence was known to be holy. There was no one who could withstand the glory of God, so he was to be approached only by the purest of pure. Thank God for sending Jesus to be that person who makes us completely pure and presentable to our holy God.

Rather than purification rituals to make us right before God, we have Jesus who lights the way and the Holy Spirit who faithfully guides us to our Maker. Enjoy being brought into God's presence today.

Holy Spirit, thank you for faithfully guiding me into the presence of my King. Thank you, Jesus, that I stand blamelessly before God because of all that you have done.

Promised Grace

I have sought Your favor with all my heart;
be gracious to me according to your promise.
PSALM 119:58 NIV

Do you wake up in the morning full of worries over decisions you need to make? Sometimes our hearts can be in turmoil because we lack knowing the right thing to do.

When God seems absent in the answers, choose to see it as an invitation to seek him more. Seek his favor with all your heart. As this Scripture says, he has promised to be gracious, so be encouraged to continue to look for his help.

Lord, I don't always know what you want me to do or say. I choose to trust in your promise and grace, knowing that even if I am unsure, you are not. I seek your favor today.

Chalkboard

The humble will see their God at work and be glad.
Let all who seek God's help be encouraged.
PSALM 69:32 NLT

Chalkboards are almost extinct these days, but if you've ever tried to write on a wet one, you'll know that the writing doesn't show up well—until the board and the chalk dry. It's an interesting process to watch the letters and words that were once faded become clear and strong. Colors become sharper and bolder.

This is how our faith can be at times. It sometimes feels like it has been wiped clear and we feel hazy just like that wet chalkboard. But God has begun to write and draw in this space. Have patience in these times because what is about to appear is beautiful, clear, and bold. God is doing something even though you can't quite make it out yet.

Lord, let me see you at work in my life today and be glad.

Pastures

Know that the Lord Himself is God;
It is He who has made us, and not we ourselves;
We are His people and the sheep of His pasture.
Psalm 100:3 nasb

In ancient times, being a sheep in a pasture meant that you belonged in a family. Sometimes the sheep pens were very small with only a few sheep, and they would sleep very near to the family.

When you think of belonging, don't think about the acres of farms of this modern world, think of an intimate setting where the shepherd and his family care deeply about each sheep. You are cared for by the great shepherd and you belong to this family of believers. Carry that sense of belonging into your day today!

Lord, thank you that you made me as a part of this family. It is not my doing but yours. I am glad to be welcomed into your arms today.

Words and Feelings

Let the words of my mouth
and the meditation of my heart
be acceptable in your sight, O Lord,
my rock and my redeemer.
PSALM 19:14 ESV

It's great to remind ourselves that God knows what we say and what we think. But this can also be a sobering reminder that we don't always say the right thing and we certainly don't think the right things! If we had to confess all the pondering that goes on in our hearts, we might be embarrassed.

God does not expect perfection in order to accept you. His acceptance is based on his complete and unconditional love for you. He wants to know you as your friend, your rock, and your redeemer. Trust him with all of you—your words and your thoughts—he accepts you!

Jesus, it is a relief to know that I am acceptable to you. I rely on your grace in those times my words and thoughts are not centered on love, knowing that you will redeem me.

Lovely Mornings

Let me hear of your unfailing love each morning,
for I am trusting you.
Show me where to walk,
for I give myself to you.
PSALM 143:8 NLT

It is beautiful to start your morning hearing of Christ's unfailing love. May that Scripture bring hope to your heart. He has unfailing love for you. In whatever you will face today, he will show you where to walk.

Giving yourself to Christ today just means that you acknowledge that he is present in all you do. Invite him to be even more present in those small thoughts, words, and decisions. Trust that he loves you enough to show you his presence throughout the day.

Lord, I am so grateful to be reminded of your unfailing love for me this morning. Thank you that you want to stand beside me and reveal your nearness to me as I walk through this day.

Reset Button

My voice you shall hear in the morning, O Lord;
In the morning I will direct it to you,
and I will look up.
PSALM 5:3 NKJV

When a computer system crashes, or an app fails to load, or you have lost your internet connection, what is your go-to way of fixing it? When we have tried everything, often it's just a matter of hitting the reset button. We turn whatever it is off for a little bit and then start it up again. Usually this is enough to get it working.

The morning can be a bit like this for us. We might have been irritated, confused, or worried when we went to bed, and a good night's sleep gives us a chance to reset in the morning. Let yourself reset. Forget the day before and start again. Direct your voice to the Lord and look up at him.

Lord, I direct my thoughts, my heart, and especially my voice to you this morning. Give me a fresh perspective for this day.

Apples and Wings

Keep me as the apple of your eye;
hide me in the shadow of your wings.
PSALM 17:8 ESV

Parents will sometimes describe their children as the apple of their eye. What they mean is that their child is at the center of their world. Rarely do good parents think about their choices and decisions without thinking about how it will affect their children. Often they will make choices entirely for their children's benefit.

Good parents protect their children at all costs. They keep them safe and secure, the way a mother hen protects her chicks underneath her wings. This is the parental kind of love that God has for you. He is the perfect parent, who is fully for you and will wholly protect you.

God, thank you for having the kind of love for me that I may never have experienced as a child. Help me to accept that you want that kind of relationship with me.

God of Nations

All the nations you have made will come and
worship before you, Lord;
they will bring glory to your name.
PSALM 86:9 NIV

It's hard to think of nations as belonging to God. Humans have been fighting for centuries to have dominion over territories, and yet it is God who created the earth and everything on it. Do you think of yourself as belonging to a certain nation? Are there other nations that you feel a dislike for? Our perspective can be challenged when we acknowledge that God is the God of all nations.

One day everyone regardless of race, ethnicity, or geographical boundary is going to worship the Lord as King. Be gracious in your thoughts toward other nations, remembering that we will all serve the same King.

King Jesus, thank you for creating and caring for every nation and every person who is part of every nation. You are the ruler of all and I pray that this nation would help to heal and not destroy other nations as part of your inclusive kingdom.

Undivided Heart

Teach me your way, LORD, that I may rely on your faithfulness;
give me an undivided heart,
that I may fear your name.
PSALM 86:11 NIV

You will have experienced what it is like to have your heart pulled in so many directions. It isn't always something bad that creates confusion about what to do or where to go, more often than not it is two good things that you have to choose between and one might not even be more right than the other. It could be a career choice, which child gets what they want over the other, or where to live for the next year.

It's in these times that you have to rely on God's faithfulness. He is ready to teach you his ways, but sometimes we have to get it wrong first before we understand more about getting it right. Give yourself grace, and keep letting God lead you.

Teach me your way, Lord, and give me an undivided heart.

Fountain of Mercy

Have mercy on me, O God, because of your unfailing love.
Because of your great compassion,
blot out the stain of my sins.
PSALM 51:1 NLT

If you don't know the great scandal of David and Bathsheba, you should read about it! This is a psalm of David after his sin of adultery: something that he got so tangled in that he certainly needed God's mercy.

It's unfortunate that in this world we have all been affected by adultery, whether our own or someone else's. God is willing to have mercy on all those who ask him to show his unfailing love. He is so full of compassion that he provided a way, through Jesus, for you to return to him.

Lord, I am so sorry for sins that I have committed that have caused great harm either to myself or to others. Please blot out the stain of my sins.

Soft Cover

He will cover you with his feathers.
He will shelter you with his wings.
His faithful promises are your armor and protection.
PSALM 91:4 NLT

If you need protection in a battle, you typically think of thick strong armor, weapons, and shields. It's interesting that this verse describes God's protection as feathers and wings! The battles that you face are likely to be emotional, mental, and spiritual. You might be struggling to keep joy at the center of your heart, you might be over analyzing a situation, or feeling burdened by a problem that you can't solve.

You need protection when you are going through these difficulties, but God's protection doesn't always look like a strong fight. Instead it looks like gentleness, kindness, and all-consuming love. This is what he covers you with as you are facing your battles. Rest in that comfort today.

Jesus, thank you for covering me in your feathers of comfort and peace. Help me to gather strength from your gentle wings of protection.

Abandoned

Even if my father and mother abandon me,
the Lord will hold me close.
Psalm 27:10 nlt

Ouch. Unfortunately, the experience of being abandoned by a father or mother is common in our world. You may feel particularly hurt by one, or both, of your parents leaving you when you were younger. It takes an incredible amount of love from others to begin to experience healing from the hurt of feeling abandoned.

If this is your experience, know that Jesus grieves with you. He is the one who hears your cries and grief, and he is the one that longs to hold you close to bring healing to your broken heart. If you have never felt this kind of abandonment, you probably know someone who has, so pray for them in this moment.

Lord, I know that you grieve when relationships don't fulfil your plan for people to experience unconditional love. Meet me and meet others in the space of feeling abandoned and hold us close.

Harvest Time

*You have given me greater joy
than those who have abundant harvests
of grain and new wine.*
PSALM 4:7 NLT

Comparison is something that we face daily. We are confronted every morning with people who have more or less than we do. We see cars on the road that are nicer than ours, people with great fashion sense, and those creative people who seem to make everything look nice.

Social media is filled with pictures of vacations, celebrations, and great achievements. It's important in these times to anchor your self-worth in the joy that you have in Jesus. Get some perspective when you feel like everyone else is doing life better than you! Be happy for them but overflow with joy for yourself because you are an heir of the King!

Lord, give me joy today as I face the many comparisons that come creeping in. Help me to be fully grounded in your eternal love.

Justice

You have maintained my just cause;
you have sat on the throne,
giving righteous judgment.
PSALM 9:4 ESV

There are so many courtroom dramas on television and each depict the judge in a different way. Sometimes a judge is kind and fair, other times they are devious and unfair. We can't assume that God is like any of these television judges. He doesn't have to be persuaded to make the right decision or stick to a manmade law. He is the absolute standard by which everything else is approved.

Aren't you glad that God's standards are purely governed by his love? Rather than worrying about his judgement, welcome it. He will always be fair to you.

Faithful God, thank you that you have maintained my cause. Thank you that you care about the injustice in this world. Help me to walk in line with you today.

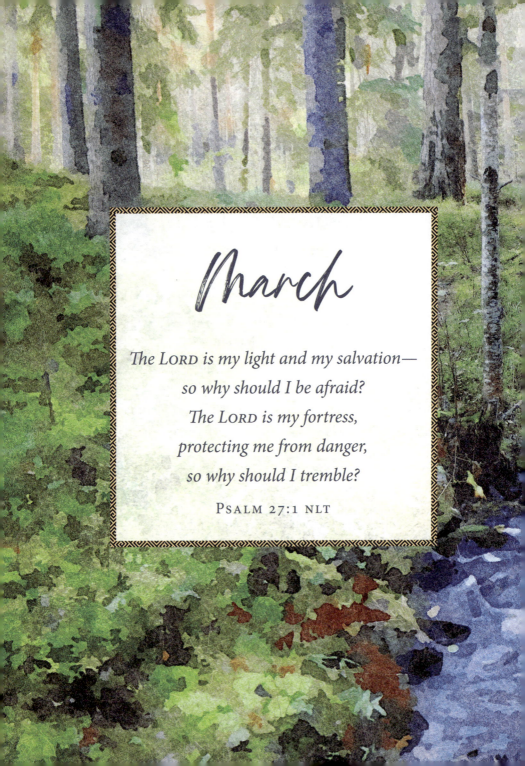

March

The LORD is my light and my salvation—
so why should I be afraid?
The LORD is my fortress,
protecting me from danger,
so why should I tremble?

PSALM 27:1 NLT

Bless Someone

*May he give you the desire of your heart
and make all your plans succeed.*
PSALM 20:4 NIV

What a beautiful Scripture to read this morning. May God give you the desire of your heart and make your plans succeed. This is a great verse for you, but could it also be for someone else in your life? Think of someone in need of encouragement today and choose to pray this blessing over that person.

It might be your mother or father, someone you know has been unwell, perhaps it's the friend with a new baby, or someone who has just started a new job. Whatever that person's situation is, pray that God would make their plans succeed!

Lord, thank you for my friends and family, for that person that came into my head as I was reading this. I ask that you would give them the desire of their heart and make their plans succeed.

Examination

Examine me, O LORD, and prove me;
try my mind and my heart.
PSALM 26:2 NKJV

Are you the type of person who prepares really well for a test or exam, or are you someone who crams at the eleventh hour? Exams make us nervous, but we are even more nervous if we are not prepared for them. It is good every once in a while to ask God to examine your heart. Of course, he already knows what is going on in your thoughts, but opening up that deeper insight into where you are really at is good.

Examine what you have been feeling and what God would say about those feelings. If you have been extremely hard on yourself for a mistake, let God into that space and realize that he would declare you free from that burden.

God, as I am preparing for my day, I open myself up to you so you can examine me deeply. Lord, try my mind and my heart and let me know if there are things I should be noticing too.

Instructions

I will instruct you and teach you in the way you should go;
I will counsel you with my loving eye on you.
PSALM 32:8 NIV

The wise person is one who listens to instruction; they continue to seek out wise ways. In the same way, the righteous person is one who wants to add to the truth that they already know.

Is your heart open to receive instruction? Do you want to add to your knowledge of the truth of God's Word? God delights in your pursuit of him and he will instruct and teach you to be wiser still.

Lord, show me when my heart has not been willing to receive your instruction. I want to know more about you, and I want to hear your truth for my life. Give me an open heart, mind, and soul to receive wisdom that can only come from you.

A Star Is Born

The Lord merely spoke, and the heavens were created.
He breathed the word, and all the stars were born.
PSALM 33:6 NLT

If you have ever had the chance to be in a remote location on a clear night, you will know what it is like to look up into the sky and marvel at the magnificent display of stars. It is such a breathtaking view—one that reminds us of the greatness of our God, the one who spoke them into existence.

Do you feel insignificant in God's great world? Remember that God has a perfect plan for this world, and you complete his plan. Lift up your eyes and know that he knows your name and that you are not missing from his plan.

God, you are so great. When I think of everything you created, I am amazed that you care about a plan for my life. Thank you that I can trust you are in control.

The Lord Is God

*Know that the LORD is God.
It is he who made us, and we are his;
we are his people, the sheep of his pasture.*
PSALM 100:3 NIV

It is comforting to know that you have a shepherd who will include you as part of the fold. You are welcomed into this family. Take a moment to reflect on the fact that not only are you a part of this family but you were created to be this family!

You were not just wandering, lost, and unknown and happened to find yourself into the fold—you have always belonged and you were always known. God created you as his family. Welcome home!

Jesus, thank you that I have always belonged to you, whether I realized that early on or am just realizing it now. Help me to walk in the assurance of belonging today.

Foundations

In the beginning you laid the foundations of the earth,
and the heavens are the work of your hands.
PSALM 102:25 NIV

Have you ever been able to watch a house being built from the foundation up? The base that goes down is what sets the size, scope, and shape of what is built upon it. A foundation isn't all that glorious, it is usually concrete, flat, and not beautiful. But it is essential to get it right.

We need foundations in our lives, but we also need to build on those foundations. This is where the real beauty happens. What would a house be without its foundation? What would a foundation be without a house? God's design for his creation is that we have both. What foundation are you laying for yourself?

Lord, help me to understand the role of having a firm foundation in my life. Teach me to put those solid things down first before I get to the handiwork.

When not If

When I am afraid,
I put my trust in you.
PSALM 56:3 NIV

A loud crash in the night. Unexpected footsteps falling uncomfortably close in a dark parking lot. A ringing phone at 3:00am. No matter how brave we think we are, certain situations quicken the pulse. We've heard, over and over, that we have nothing to fear if we walk with God, but let's be honest: certain situations are scary!

You might be anxious about today. Perhaps there is a big event that you are a part of, or maybe you have to have a difficult conversation. Maybe you are just nervous because you don't know what the day will bring. The Psalms say that you can trust God with all your heart. Trust him today.

Lord, I don't know what is going to happen today, but I make the decision right now to trust in you with all my heart. Give me peace for my day ahead.

To the Hills

I look up to the hills,
but where does my help come from?
PSALM 121:1 NCV

Depending on the type of person you are, you may not be very good at asking for help. There are those who like to be helpers: they do best serving others because they feel capable and useful. Then there are those who gladly accept service any time they are given the opportunity. Neither is better than the other, and both have their positive elements.

Can you easily ask for help? God asks you to take a chance on the people he's intricately placed in your life. You'll be amazed at how much stronger you feel when you're leaning on those who want to carry the load with you.

Lord, I can often ask you for help, but I struggle to ask others. Thank you that life is never truly independent and that you created people to depend on one another. Bring some help into my life today.

Life's Journey

You will show me the path of life;
in your presence is fullness of joy;
at your right hand are pleasures forevermore.

PSALM 16:11 NKJV

Though we commonly associate the words fear and fright with one another, they don't mean the same thing. Having a fear of the Lord means we respect him. It means we are in awe of him. He is, in fact, a God of great joy. When we seek to be fully in his presence, we can find that joy.

Our Father wants you to experience his joy. Pleasures forevermore? Let's sign up for that! Shake off any old notions of dread or apprehension you may feel about being in his presence and seek the path of life he has set for you. He is a source of great delight. Rejoice in that knowledge today.

Father, I am in awe of who you are and of what you have done. Give me joy today as I respect your greatness and goodness in my life.

Without Limit

Your faithfulness flows from one generation to the next;
all that you created sits firmly in place to testify of you.
PSALM 119:90 TPT

What's the oldest thing you own? How long have you had it, and what does it mean to you? Whether a decades-old diamond ring, twenty-year-old car, or a tattered baby blanket hanging together by threads, you probably know it won't last forever. How about your longest relationship? How many years have you been connected through good and bad?

One way you decide where to place your faith is longevity. History matters. You can carry on the faithfulness of the generations as you go about your day. Take Jesus with you in your heart and actions.

Lord, thank you that this life in you is the most real thing I can ever know. When I doubt you, let me remind myself that your love has been around since the beginning of time.

Hunger

Poor people will eat until they are full;
those who look to the LORD will praise him.
May your hearts live forever!
PSALM 22:26 NCV

When was the last time you exclaimed, "I'm starving!"? How about, "I'm so full!"? Many of us say both things in a week. Occasionally at the beginning and end of a single meal. Clearly when we examine these terms literally, and in the greater context of a hungry world, we are not starving if we have the means to become full only minutes later. Chances are we don't even begin to know what that kind of hunger feels like.

So, what are we saying? We are recognizing, by the empty, gnawing feeling in our bellies, an unmet need. As you take some time out of your busy day, make sure to fill your heart with Jesus so you won't be empty.

Lord, thank you that you have given me fullness of life. I praise you because you have met all my needs. Fill my heart with you today.

Small Stuff

What are mere mortals that you should think about them,
human beings that you should care for them?
PSALM 8:4 NLT

If you have ever watched a scientific program about our universe, you will likely feel overwhelmed by how colossal and complex our universe and surrounding galaxies are! It can make humans seem tiny and insignificant when you consider that as a planet, earth is nothing in comparison to the vastness of the rest of the cosmos!

What are mere mortals that God would think about us; why would he care? Genesis tells us that God made us in his image—that has to be pretty special. He created us with intention; he created us to be like him and to live in relationship with him. He created us for love. Let his love for you overwhelm you today.

Lord, I'm not sure how significant I am in light of this universe, and yet your Word says you adore me! Thank you that you are so great and yet so personal.

Creation Care

You care for the land and water it; you enrich it abundantly.
The streams of God are filled with water to
provide the people with grain,
for so you have ordained it.
PSALM 65:9 NIV

You don't have to be a tree hugger these days to be part of taking care of the land and the water. Human intelligence has progressed our lives significantly, but unfortunately much of it has been at the expense of creating a whole lot of mess.

God didn't create the world for us to abuse but to enjoy and take care of. If he cares about the land, water, and soil, then as his image bearers we need to have that same amount of care. The land is crying out for redemption, and we can be a part of the plan. What changes can you implement that will make a small but positive different to our natural environment?

God, thank you for your beautiful creation. I know you have asked us to take care of it and I want to be part of your plan for its redemption. Please show me what I can do to help make a difference.

Vows

Make thankfulness your sacrifice to God,
and keep the vows you made to the Most High.
PSALM 50:4 NLT

In ancient times, sacrifices were the way to please and appease the Gods. The Israelites would go to great lengths to find favor with God through sacrifices, yet God was never about the sacrifice. He was about the heart behind it.

Instead of requiring burnt animals, God asks for a sacrifice of thanks. As you get ready for the coming day, don't rush around thinking that everything you do is more important than a thankful heart. Stop for a minute and offer up a prayer of gratitude to God.

Father, thank you for the many blessings I have in my life. I am grateful for being accepted into your family. I am blessed with provision and meaningful relationships. Thank you!

Societal Norms

*Blessed is the one who does not walk in step with the wicked
or stand in the way that sinners take
or sit in the company of mockers.*
PSALM 1:1 NIV

What is your definition of a wicked person? The language of this verse brings our thoughts to the extremes of evil, yet it is simply referring to those who do not know or love God. In essence, this is the world around us; it's the people we see in the grocery store, the parents we meet at school, the person who sits next to you at work.

How often do we fall in step with societal norms? Be mindful of the way you use your language and your humor and consider if you are pursuing the goals and expectations set by those around you. Our conformity to the world can come in small and subtle ways. Refresh your thoughts with the spirit of Christ so you can fall in step with him.

God, it is so easy to become like those I spend a lot of time with. Please help me to guard my heart, and let my words and actions be reflective of your love and grace.

Compassion

The LORD is compassionate and gracious,
Slow to anger and abounding in mercy.
PSALM 103:8 NASB

Consider the Israelites wandering in the desert: God had rescued them out of bondage and went before them in a pillar of fire, providing for their every need and protecting them. What did they offer back to him? Complaints.

God loves his children regardless of their sin, their past, and their failings. We aren't dealt with as we deserve; rather, according to his great love for us. Can we say the same about how we treat those around us? Are we compassionate, slow to anger, and full of love? Or are we offended, impatient, and aggravated?

Lord, I want to be more like you. Give me grace for others. Help me to be slow to anger and to show compassion that is beyond human capability. Thank you, Holy Spirit, for your supernatural power in my life.

Rewarded

*The LORD has rewarded me according to my righteousness,
according to the cleanness of my hands in his sight.*
PSALM 18:24 ESV

What do you think of when you hear the word purity? Perhaps a nun in her convent—someone who keeps herself completely untouched by the temptations of the world—an innocent child, or a great religious figure?

Often when we think about purity we think of a lack of obvious, outward sin. But both purity and impurity are birthed in the heart and developed in the mind long before they become expressed in action. Our purity is measured not in what we do or what we have done but in the hidden places of our heart's attitudes and our mind's wanderings.

Lord, help me to have a pure attitude today and to set my mind on the good and true things that are in my life. Let me walk in your righteousness.

Waiting

I waited and waited and waited some more;
patiently, knowing God would come through for me.
PSALM 40:1 TPT

Let's be honest: we're not that good at waiting for anything these days. Yet, the reality is that waiting is a necessary part of life. We wait for people, we wait for events, and we wait for desires to be fulfilled. But do we recognize that waiting might also apply to our emotional lives? Do we hold on to hope that we can be rescued from a troubled heart?

Do you feel as though your emotions are on slippery ground or that your thoughts are stuck in the miry clay? Are you willing to wait patiently for the great rescuer to lift you up and place your feet on solid ground? Take a moment today to ask God for his help. Recognize the necessity of waiting and trust God to come to the rescue.

Lord, I need your help today. I'm not sure what this day is going to look like, but I trust that you will be with me.

All I Need

The LORD is all I need.
He takes care of me.
PSALM 16:5 NCV

God created us as we are, and he declared his creation to be good. Furthermore, he has given us the gift of always being near. To know that Jesus is right next to us all the time is really all we need.

This is the contentment the Bible speaks of. Are you able to realize God's presence with you today, and let that fill you with contentment?

Lord, thank you for what I have been given. Sometimes I feel like I need more. I am not always content with how much money I have, or what my house looks like, or even the clothes that I own. But I am thankful that you have given me food, a roof over my head, and clothing and that is enough for me.

Meditate It Away

Be angry, and do not sin.
PSALM 4:4 NKJV

Have you ever been mad enough that you actually tremble? Sometimes we can be overwhelmed with emotions of anger— sometimes for good reasons and sometimes not. Whatever the reason, the Bible speaks of the need to take some time out to calm down.

God is not overly concerned with the fact that we get angry. He understands the emotions of his creation. However, acting out in anger never achieves anything good. The Psalmist knew that sin often followed anger. Fortunately, we are given a helpful technique in how to handle our anger.

God, I hope that I won't have anything to be angry about, but chances are there are probably things that are going to bother me. I pray if there is anything that upsets me today you would help me to process my emotions in the right way. Let me bring my heart to you in honesty, and let you deal with the rest.

Don't Fall

*Those who love your instructions
have great peace and do not stumble.*
PSALM 119:165 NLT

We are all well acquainted with stress. There are so many things in our lives that cause us to be worried, pressured, and anxious. The world constantly presents us with unknowns and predicaments that steal our joy and rob our peace.

You might be facing some predicaments today. Spend time in God's presence, letting his peace wash over your heart. Focus on his truth and capability rather than your problems and incapacity. God is able to take everything that is troubling you and exchange it for peace that is beyond what you can imagine.

God, you are the most loving father, and you care about my wellbeing. I choose to follow your instructions, knowing that it will bring me peace.

Heart Failure

My flesh and my heart fail;
but God is the strength of my heart and my portion forever.
PSALM 73:26 NKJV

Have you ever had a moment where you've felt completely out of control? A car accident, a diagnosis, or some other frightening instance? There are moments in our lives when our own flesh fails us. We recognize in a flash that we are no longer in control of our outcome, and it terrifies us.

In that moment, when control is lost and fear overcomes, there is one thing you can know for certain. God is your strength; he never loses control. When your life, and the outcome of it, is ripped from your hands, it's still resting firmly in his grasp. He is your portion. He is enough. Release yourself today into the control of the only one who will never lose control.

Heavenly Father, when my heart feels weak, I thank you that you are my strength. I thank you that you will never fail me. I choose to rely on your strength today.

Practice Peace

Keep turning your back on every sin,
and make "peace" your life motto.
Practice being at peace with everyone.
PSALM 34:14 TPT

It can be easy to get emotionally entangled in arguments or tense situations. We are naturally curious, and we take great interest in what's going on in others' lives.

Oftentimes our curiosity is driven by an honest fascination with people and relationships, but if we are not careful, we can easily cross the fine line into gossip and—for lack of a better term— drama. Turn your back on this temptation today and choose peace instead.

Lord, at times I am tempted to engage in gossip and words that do not bring life or peace into situations. I am sorry when I do this and ask for your grace to help me become a person of peace.

Promise of Hope

Your promise revives me;
it comforts me in all my troubles.
PSALM 119:50 NLT

Grief is a strange thing. It shows up in the oddest of places. As time passes, it becomes threaded into your life in a subtle way you don't quite notice at first. When you smile and feel real joy but at the same moment tears spring to your eyes, that's when you know that grief is not absent even in happiness.

It is comforting to know that the God of comfort is nearby. He waits for us to share our pain with him and he is ready to give us everything we need in each moment of grief we experience. Reach out to him when you need comfort for your troubles.

Father, I know that you care deeply for me and that you also care about my pain. I ask for comfort in the times that seem the hardest to bear, and I ask for your joy even in the middle of difficult times.

Show and Tell

Tell me in the morning about your love, because I trust you.
Show me what I should do, because my prayers go up to you.
PSALM 143:8 NCV

There are many verses in the Bible that talk about morning prayer. Jesus himself set an example by getting up early and going to a quiet place to talk with God. There is something about the morning that God values. Mornings symbolize new life, strong hope, and fresh beginnings—all things that we know God is passionate about.

When we seek God in the morning, we consecrate the first moments of the day. By coming and placing ourselves at his feet before we do anything else, we put him first in our hearts, souls, and minds.

Lord Jesus, I put you first in my heart and mind this morning. I set my eyes on you and ask you to calm the storm of the day as I follow you into it.

Grace Fountain

O Lord, you are so good, so ready to forgive,
so full of unfailing love for all who ask for your help.
Psalm 86:5 NLT

Sometimes there is heaviness in your heart that you just can't shake. It might not be anything in particular that is troubling you, but you just can't quite see the good side of life.

Instead of relying on that first cup of coffee to get you motivated, read this verse over and over and let the words encourage and lift your spirit. God is so good, so ready to forgive and so full of unfailing love. Ask for his help today and be sure that you will receive it.

Father, thank you for reminding me of your goodness. Forgive me for any bitterness or complaint in my heart and show me your unfailing love. Help me as I head into this day.

Unburdening

Here's what I've learned through it all:
Leave all your cares and anxieties at the feet of the Lord,
and measureless grace will strengthen you.
PSALM 55:22 TPT

This life is always going to hand us some pretty big burdens. We have responsibilities for so many things. You might need to finish an assignment, deliver a work presentation, or take care of a sick child. Sometimes we face even harder burdens like a health crisis or loss of a job. Cares and anxieties are real, yet Jesus wants us to give them to him. What does that mean to you?

Leaving your cares with Christ might simply mean that you have someone to pour your heart out to. It is often said that we unburden by sharing our thoughts and emotions with others. Well, Jesus is ready to hear everything—you don't have to hold back! Spend some time bringing your cares and anxieties to him today.

Jesus, thank you that you listen to all my worries. I bring them to you now and accept your grace and strength to face the day.

Reaching Beyond

Your love is so extravagant it reaches to the heavens,
Your faithfulness so astonishing it stretches to the sky!
PSALM 57:10 TPT

Have you ever seen anything come close to reaching the heavens? The tallest tree might look spectacular, and the highest skyscraper appears an amazing feat, and yet these things are nothing in comparison to the mercy of God!

You might not think of yourself as a judgmental person, but it's in our human nature to analyze or evaluate others' behaviors and attitudes especially in comparison with our own. When you feel like you might be doing that let the grandeur of God's mercy help you to put things in perspective. His love is simply so much greater than ours.

Lord, give me your perspective as I walk into my day, declaring your mercy that reaches the heavens.

Before and Beside

I have set the LORD always before me;
because he is at my right hand,
I shall not be shaken.
PSALM 16:8 ESV

What might it mean to set the Lord before you? This morning, or as you are reading this, you are doing just that: taking some time out of your day to consider your Creator and to focus on your relationship with him.

As you think about him before you, remember also, to place him beside you. Think of him as your constant companion—the one who is there to steady you throughout the day. Approach this day with confidence, knowing that he is near.

Jesus, thank you for being so present with me. I choose to set you before me this day, so I can remain guided and anchored by your hand.

Eternal Song

I will sing my song to the Lord as long as I live!
Every day I will sing my praises to God.
PSALM 104:33 TPT

Are you the kind of person who loves to sing, or someone who just appreciates listening? The gift of song is that it is another expression of your thoughts and feelings about something or someone.

Think of the ways that you best express yourself. Is it writing, speaking, walking? Perhaps it really is singing? Whatever your expression, direct it toward the Lord this morning. You'll find it will give you great perspective as you start your day.

Holy Spirit, thank you for the gift of expression. Thank you that I have many ways to share my heart with you. In this moment, I direct my creativity toward you and express my own song in whatever shape that forms.

Perfect

It is God who arms me with strength,
and makes my way perfect.
PSALM 18:32 NKJV

Have you ever been stuck for words, lacking the ability to find exactly how to get across your point? We don't always have all the answers and sometimes we just need the humility to admit that we don't get it.

This verse is a good reminder that God is the source of your strength. When you are going through a difficult time or have a tough decision to make, you don't have to rely on your own understanding because it is not perfect. Instead rely on God as your source. He will guide your mind and your heart toward the right thing.

Jesus, this morning I choose to bring my anxieties about my situation to you. Thank you for arming me with your strength and showing me your perfect ways.

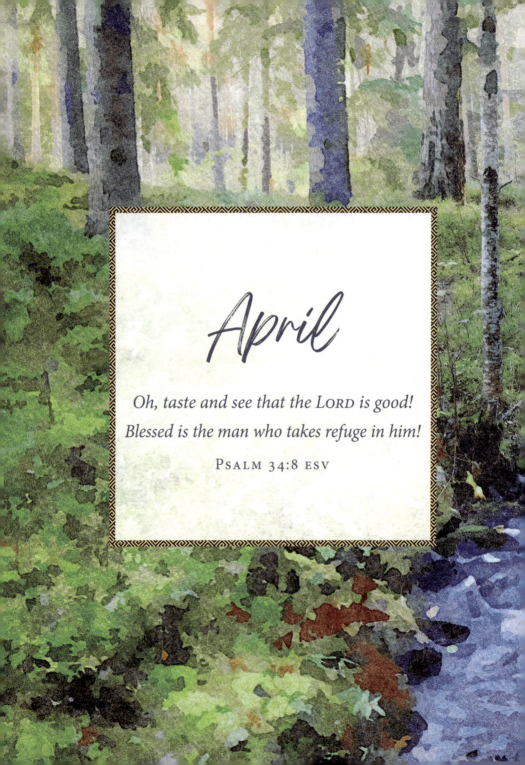

April

Oh, taste and see that the Lord is good!

Blessed is the man who takes refuge in him!

Psalm 34:8 esv

Paths of Righteousness

He restores my soul;
He leads me in the paths of righteousness
for His name's sake.
PSALM 23:3 NKJV

What was your mood like when you woke up this morning? Were you brimming with joy about the day ahead, or were you irritated for having to get up so early? Maybe you haven't had your morning coffee yet, or you haven't eaten breakfast and you're not feeling like being polite to the people in your house.

This is the real world and you aren't expected to be "righteous" every step of the way! The idea in this verse is that you have a loving friend in Jesus and he will guide you in the right paths, whether that is where you go, or the attitude with which you deal with people and situations. Don't be so hard on yourself; lean on your shepherd!

Jesus, thank you for your grace that allows me to be kind to myself, knowing that I don't always do things right and trusting that you will still make good of my intentions to do right.

You Are Near

Even when I walk through the darkest valley,
I will not be afraid, for you are close beside me.
Your rod and your staff protect and comfort me.
PSALM 23:4 NLT

Valleys are part of the journey of life. In the physical world, we often have to walk through valleys to get to greener pastures. If you are experiencing some kind of low in your life right now, remember that your shepherd is near to you and will guide you along in those particularly rough patches.

Allow yourself to envision what is beyond the valley: fresher waters, calmer weather, greener pastures. Let the hope of what is on the other side make you stronger as you weather the storm, knowing that you have your Savior beside you all along the way.

Jesus, as I face valleys in my life, give me vision that sees beyond the troubles, knowing that you are there to protect and comfort me along the way to better things.

Feasting

You prepare a feast for me in the presence of my enemies.
You honor me by anointing my head with oil.
My cup overflows with blessings.
PSALM 23:5 NLT

You probably aren't physically preparing for battle today, but in the days of these Scriptures, battle was all too common. When facing enemies, it was important to have the right nourishment so you could have the strength to face the fight.

You won't have enemies or probably need to fight, but you do need strength to face the hurdles that will come across your path. Make sure you are nourished by his Word each day so you are equipped for the day.

Lord, thank you for the gift of Scripture that brings me hope and strength. As I read your words, bring them to life and remind me throughout the day of the hope that knowing you brings.

Forever with God

Surely your goodness and love will follow me all the days of my life,
and I will dwell in the house of the LORD forever.
PSALM 23:6 NIV

Any long journey has its ups and downs. Even the best holiday will involve a few valley moments. Throughout the years, however, people with Christ in their lives have been able to attest to the goodness of God throughout all their circumstances.

This is why the writers of the psalms can confidently say, "Surely goodness and love will follow me." At the end of it all, you will look back and know that God has been good to you.

Jesus, I choose to be positive about the future and know that your goodness will follow me. Help me to gain perspective of what goodness might mean. I know things might not always be easy, but you will be good to me.

Patient God

The LORD is compassionate and gracious,
slow to anger, abounding in love.
PSALM 103:8 NIV

What is on the agenda, today? We wake up and have a lot of things to do even before we head out the door. Sometimes in our rush, we get irritable and ungracious when things don't go smoothly.

Our need to get things done leaves us feeling rushed and quick to anger. It might help to know that God is not like this at all. His nature is love first and love always. This means that he is slow to anger and really, really quick to accept you—warts and all!

Lord, sometimes I don't feel like I deserve your compassion, and yet, you love me with all of your being. Instead of feeling guilty about my anger, help me to reflect on how much grace you have for me, and let this inspire me to be more gracious to others.

Pure Gold

The words of the LORD are flawless,
like silver purified in a crucible,
like gold refined seven times.
PSALM 12:6 NIV

Gold and silver are precious metals, and yet they become beautiful over a process of time and intense purification involving heat and separation. Scriptures illustrate God's words as silver and gold. His words are precious and should be considered rare and valuable. Often, we are not ready for his words. We lack understanding of the beauty and wisdom that comes from truly understanding his ways.

God's words are pure, but our hearing might not be! Be ready, even today, to let your understanding be refined.

Jesus, thank you that I can trust your words are right and pure. Give me eyes to truly see and ears to fully understand. I need fresh revelation.

O People

Trust in him at all times, you people;
pour out your hearts before him.
God is our refuge.
PSALM 62:8 CSB

We like to spend time on our personal relationship with God, and yet there is more to our faith than just ourselves. We were created to be in community with one another and one really important benefit of a close community is that we can be encouraged, or encourage others, in times of distress.

Think of the last time you felt really anxious or discouraged and reflect on who you were able to share those feelings with. Together we can pour out our hearts to him. We are all on this journey, not just individually, but walking alongside each other. Take a moment today to encourage the people you are walking with through life.

God, thank you for the people you have put in my life that I can be in community with. Help me to be intentional about developing close relationships with those who encourage me in my faith and with those I need to encourage.

Cheer Up

When the cares of my heart are many,
your consolations cheer my soul.
PSALM 94:19 ESV

The variety of translations of this verse are good at describing what anxiety feels like: it is many cares of your heart, it is great worry, it is when doubts fill your mind. You might be someone who has struggled with anxiety for most of your life, but even if you haven't, you likely have felt the weight of anxiety at times.

Perhaps you are facing work or study deadlines, maybe you are struggling with the discipline of one of your children. You might be having difficulties in your marriage, or you are feeling alone and uncertain about what your next move might be. All of these cares weigh you down. Share them with Jesus; he wants to console you and bring cheer to your soul.

God, thank you for a new morning. Even though I may have woken up with a lot of cares and concerns, I pray I would be able to trust that you will help me sort out the things that are within my control, and to let go of the things that are not.

Smells Good

May my prayer be set before you like incense;
may the lifting up of my hands be like the evening sacrifice.
PSALM 141:2 NIV

The thought of trying to appease the gods is a little foreign to us, but in the ancient times, rituals were all part of the people's worship. You probably don't burn incense for any spiritual reason, but you do pray, and that is a ritual—an act of your worship. Lifting up your hands during a worship song is another ritual.

There is something about showing God praise through your expression. God gave you a mind, body, and senses to be used for praising him. Speak out your prayers to him as your act of worship.

God, I praise you for the great King that you are but also as the lover of my soul. I am so thankful that my life belongs to you.

In Your Hands

My times are in your hand;
deliver me from the hand of my enemies and persecutors.
PSALM 31:15 NRSV

Time is precious. If there are too many demands on our time we feel out of control or stressed. It might be a relief, or a little bit strange, to try and view our time with a different perspective. Instead of feeling ownership over time, we can think of God as not only the author of all time, but the author of our time.

If you realize that time has been given to you as a gift from God, then perhaps you can relax knowing that you don't have to be in control of it. Your times are in his hands and he knows what you need and what you can handle. He will deliver you from trouble.

Thank you, Father, for creating this time and this space for me to live in. Help me to see time as a gift and to use it wisely. Help me to relinquish my feeling of ownership of this time and instead offer it to you for your glory.

Release Me

Deliver me, my God, from the hand of the wicked,
from the grasp of those who are evil and cruel.
PSALM 71:4 NIV

Hopefully you are not the person who is praying this prayer right now, but there's always a chance that someone out there is. It's a sad reality that people suffer, and often at the hands of other people. That's why we have a God who was determined to redeem this world, and he chose to do that through his Son.

Jesus suffered at the hands of hatred and cruelty and he defeated that evil by enduring it and then rising again to new life. This is the hope that we have for humanity. Instead of despairing at the evil in this world, be hopeful about the promise that God has made a path for redemption.

Jesus, thank you for giving humanity hope that one day all evil will be gone and creation will be restored. I pray for all of those who are suffering because of cruelty and I ask for you to deliver them. Let the world see your light and truth.

Radiance

Look to him, and be radiant;
so your faces shall never be ashamed.
PSALM 34:5 NRSV

Life is full of decisions—big and small. Your personality might be one that likes to make swift decisions, or you may be someone who deliberates carefully over the right choice. Our brains are wired differently in this process.

God designed you uniquely, yet he never intended that you would have to make decisions on your own. Are you facing some important decisions right now? Look to God to help you in the process; he knows what will make you shine!

Lord, be with me as I make decisions today, whether they have small or big consequences. Help me to practice looking to you when I need help so I can rely on you more and more.

Good Father

As a father shows compassion to his children,
so the LORD shows compassion to those who fear him.
PSALM 103:13 ESV

Regardless of how beautifully or imperfectly your earthly father showed his love, your heavenly Father's love is utterly boundless. Rest in that thought a moment.

There is nothing you can do to change how he feels about you. It's easy to forget we are already perfectly loved. Our Father loves us more than we can imagine. And he would do anything for us. Remember this throughout your day and allow it to give you confidence for everything you face.

Lord, thank you that you care so much about me. You have unfailing compassion for me. I want to approach this day as a child who knows that I am loved even if I make mistakes.

Hungry

He satisfies the longing soul,
and the hungry soul he fills with good things.
PSALM 107:9 ESV

The appetite is a funny thing. Our bodies have the ability to communicate hunger to our brains, and our brains then cause us to seek out a solution to the problem. When we are genuinely hungry, we look for food that will fill our stomachs and quiet our hunger.

Our souls have appetites also, but we so easily fill our time and energy with the world's entertainment. We fill ourselves up with things that will never be able to satisfy and leave little room for the only one who can. Watch what you fill your soul with today. Feast on the goodness of God so you don't remain hungry.

Lord, when I get hungry today, remind me also to hunger for you. Help me to fill that hunger with goodness and not evil, so I am spiritually fit and healthy.

Beautiful Union

Love and faithfulness meet together;
righteousness and peace kiss each other.
PSALM 85:10 NIV

A mug of hot chocolate on a cold winter's day. A mother duck and her duckling floating effortlessly across the pond. Some things fit together so beautifully. Love meets wondrously with faithfulness because love is the reason to be faithful. Peace comes exquisitely after a right choice is made.

There is so much harmony and balance when we let one good thing guide our decisions. It just naturally flows into another good emotion. Be encouraged, today, to choose faithfulness and righteousness. Be ready to feel overwhelming love and unexplainable joy as you walk in the fruit of the Spirit.

Holy Spirit, guide me into faithfulness and righteousness in all of my decisions today and especially in all of my relationships. Let me begin to experience the love and peace of having a heart that is led by you.

Free from Chains

He brought them out of darkness and the shadow of death,
and broke their chains in pieces.

PSALM 107:14 NKJV

There is a chance to start over—every day if we need to. From the inside out, we can be transformed and our hearts renewed. We can essentially remake ourselves with the help, healing, and transformative nature of Christ!

Jesus died on the cross to promise you a life free from the bondage of sin, free from hopelessness, free from any chains that try to trap you. In Christ, you are set free. Embrace this promise today.

Lord, I want to start this day new. I seek to follow your heart in everything that I do, and I thank you that you will not be far from me.

Music for the Soul

*Let us come before him with thanksgiving
and extol him with music and song.*
PSALM 95:2 NIV

When was the last time you gave yourself over fully to a time of worship? Not just singing along to the words in church, not just bowing your head in prayer, but letting yourself be completely consumed by the presence of the Lord? Music is such a gift, and it is little wonder that we want to express ourselves in a way that reflects the Creator of music!

Take some quiet time today to listen to music and allow God's divine presence to wash over you, filling every crevice of your being. Revel in the time that you have with him, worshiping him in whatever way feels natural to you.

Lord, I worship you with my whole heart this morning. Give me time in my day to reflect on how truly wonderful you are.

Posture

Come, let's worship and bow down;
let's kneel before the LORD our Maker.
PSALM 95:6 CSB

Worship comes in many forms. It is not just songs and dancing, worship is the way that we direct our hearts, minds, and posture toward our maker. It might feel more appropriate sometimes to acknowledge how great our Lord is by kneeling before him. This simple act is not just about submission or subservience. It is an act of acknowledging that God has authority over his creation, and over you, if you will allow him.

Let God take care of you instead of worrying about how you will take care of yourself today. You don't have to let him take control, but you might be more at peace if you do!

Maker of all, I bow down before you out of reverence for your creativity and dominion over everything. I want you to direct my heart and mind today.

Open Up

That my soul may sing praise to You and not be silent.
Lord my God, I will give thanks to You forever.
Psalm 30:12 nasb

Have you ever felt the song of your heart praising the Lord? No words may come, no verses, no chorus, and yet your very being feels as though it may burst from the music inside you. You are not alone! Even the very heavens praise him in this way.

Break forth into your song! Allow your heart to feel the words even if you cannot fully form them. Give God all your praises today. He is so deserving of them. Let your heart be a celebration of your love for Jesus. Give in to the melody of worship inside you.

Jesus, I worship you this morning. My heart is full of your splendor, and I want that to spill out into my day.

Word Wise

How can a young person stay on the path of purity?
By living according to your word.
PSALM 119:9 NIV

We are met with a lot of opposition in our daily pursuit of Christ. We get side tracked so easily with the things of this world, our own emotional struggles, and our war with sin. Without the truth of the living, active Word of God, we are defenseless to successfully live the Christian life.

The Word of God is our best defense against hopelessness, fear, and sin—and at the same time it's our best offensive weapon against temptation, lies, and the enemy of our souls. Use it to guide you on the path of purity today.

Lord, thank you for your Scriptures; they bring life to my heart and wisdom to my thoughts. Keep my way pure as I live by your Word.

Take the Leap

The LORD is my strength and my shield;
my heart trusts in him, and he helps me.
My heart leaps for joy, and with my song I praise him.
PSALM 28:7 NIV

Most great things in life take some risk. We probably can each say that we've taken some pretty dumb chances in life, but we have also taken some incredible ones. Some of our risks end in disaster, but others in sheer beauty.

One thing all risk has in common is that it teaches us something. We never walk away unchanged. And while stepping out and taking the risk itself is scary, we discover our own bravery in it.

Teach me to take measured risks for you today, Lord. I know that you want me to live a life of adventure, and when you ask me to step out, I know that it will be a risk worth taking.

Infinite Resource

Great is our Lord and abundant in strength;
His understanding is infinite.
PSALM 147:5 NASB

When you approach God to ask for help in resisting temptation or for forgiveness for sin you've given into, do you feel ashamed? Do you feel like God couldn't possibly understand how you fell into that sin once again?

We know that Jesus was tempted to sin while he was here on earth, but we also know that he never gave into it. Because he experienced temptation, he has great compassion toward us when we struggle with the desire to sin.

I am so glad that you understand what I am going through, Lord. At times I feel like nobody understands or cares, but I am reminded today that you have infinite understanding of my complicated heart.

Willing to Listen.

My people would not listen to me;
Israel would not submit to me.
PSALM 81:11 NIV

Stubbornness is a tricky attribute. There is often no opening for conversation with a stubborn person. They have their own idea about how things should be done, and they aren't usually willing to listen to the advice of others.

We all tend to be stubborn in certain ways. Unfortunately, our stubbornness sometimes comes out toward God. We feel his Spirit gently advising us, but we rationalize it away in our heads instead of allowing it to guide our hearts. God can do more in a month with a life fully surrendered to him than he can do in years with a life that's holding back.

God, I am sorry for holding back from the things that you have asked me to do. I am afraid, embarrassed, and just a bit stubborn. I don't want to let my stubborn heart get in the way, so help me to trust you and let go so you can do what you want with my life.

Waking and Sleeping

I lay down and slept;
I awoke, for the LORD sustains me.
PSALM 3:5 NASB

There is always something to worry about, isn't there? Whether it's health, finances, relationships, or details, there are many unknowns in life that can easily keep us worrying. But what if we stopped worrying? What if we could trust completely that God would take care of us and our loved ones. God is our rock and he alone will sustain us.

There will be moments when the rug feels as though it's been pulled out from under you, and there is nothing to do but despair. In the moments that you can't control, you can trust. You can rest your soul, your mind, and your body in the hands of the one who has the power to sustain you.

Lord, today I face the unknown. Let me rest in the knowledge that you will sustain me.

Count on Me

*Those who know Your name will put their trust in you;
for You, Lord, have not forsaken those who seek you.*
Psalm 9:10 NKJV

It feels easier to trust God in the big moments, the desperate moments. But what about the everyday moments? The times that we grab hold of control and want to do it all ourselves. In those moments, we can press into him without restraint.

Let go, cry out to him, ask him to carry you. And he will. The everyday moments that might feel crooked will be straightened. He will carry you as he promises.

Jesus, thank you for being a good shepherd. Help me to seek out your ways today, in the everyday decisions. I know you don't need to tell me what exactly to do but help me to be like you so I reflect your nature to others around me.

Sacred Places

He who dwells in the secret place of the Most High
shall abide under the shadow of the Almighty.
PSALM 91:1 NKJV

Have you ever been awake when you think no one else is? Maybe you had an early morning flight, and you feel you are the only person who could possibly be stirring at that hour. It feels kind of magical, doesn't it? It's like you have an unshared secret.

Regardless of you being a night owl, morning person, or somewhere in between, there is peace that comes with meeting Jesus in secret—when your world has stopped for a bit. You need spiritual food to conquer each day, so make sure you partake of it.

Jesus, I'm glad to have this moment with you. Thank you that even a small amount of time with you gives me the courage to face this day with confidence and serenity.

Healer

He heals the broken hearted
and binds up their wounds.
PSALM 147:3 NIV

Whether you are carrying pain and suffering from past abuse or tragedy, or you've more recently been hurt, run toward the one who heals.

There is no requirement or need too great; God will piece you back together. Your offering of praise to him is beautiful and he will turn your mourning into joy.

Lord, I come to you as a person who has been broken and hurt by others. Sometimes I feel this pain more acutely than other times, but wherever I am with this, Lord, you know the things that have really torn my heart. Give me peace today, knowing that you are helping me to forgive and become whole again.

Rescuer

The righteous person faces many troubles,
but the LORD comes to the rescue each time.
PSALM 34:19 NLT

Scripture says it loud and clear: we can expect to face trouble! What do you do when you face trouble of any kind? Do you hide from pain, run from it, or get angry about it? There's something about trouble that sends us into survival mode. We don't like to feel uncomfortable; we don't want emotional or physical pain.

Perhaps you could look at your troubles in a different light today. Whatever is troubling you is probably causing you to do a bit of soul searching, and you might even need to reach out to Jesus and ask him to rescue you. This could be a good thing; it could be a wonderful thing! Allow yourself to reflect on why you are feeling troubled and pour your heart out to Jesus. See your trouble as leading you to the arms of your Savior.

Jesus, I don't like when trouble is at my doorstep. I feel afraid, I feel embarrassed, and I feel alone. I'm reaching out to you now, asking for you to rescue me.

Broken

Be merciful to me, Lord, for I am in distress;
my eyes grow weak with sorrow,
my soul and body with grief.
PSALM 31:9 NIV

Grief shows up in unexpected places and times; it doesn't follow a formula, and it looks very different for everyone. It's important that we are able to express how we are feeling, when we are feeling it.

As time passes and life goes on, we must learn to bear all of our varying emotions in sync. We can smile, we can laugh, and we can be perfectly happy, but the ache of grief is still there deep down. We don't forget it, but we don't betray that which we grieve by smiling either.

Father, I know that you care deeply for me. When I am in distress and full of sorrow, fill me with hope for a new day—a day without pain and suffering. You have promised that day will come.

Be Considerate

Happy are those who consider the poor;
the Lord delivers them in the day of trouble.
PSALM 41:1 NRSV

As Christ followers, we are his image bearers; the visible expression of an invisible God. In order to express the heart of the Father, we have to know what is on his heart. God tells us in Scripture that he cares deeply about the least of these: the orphan, the widow, the poor, the needy.

We cannot preach Christ to someone who is needy while leaving them in their need. Our words will not communicate the love of our Father unless accompanied by the actions that make him tangible to them.

Lord, let me show my faith in action toward those in need. Holy Spirit, guide me to the needs of others, whether it is someone close to me or far away. Help me to respond quickly to help others today.

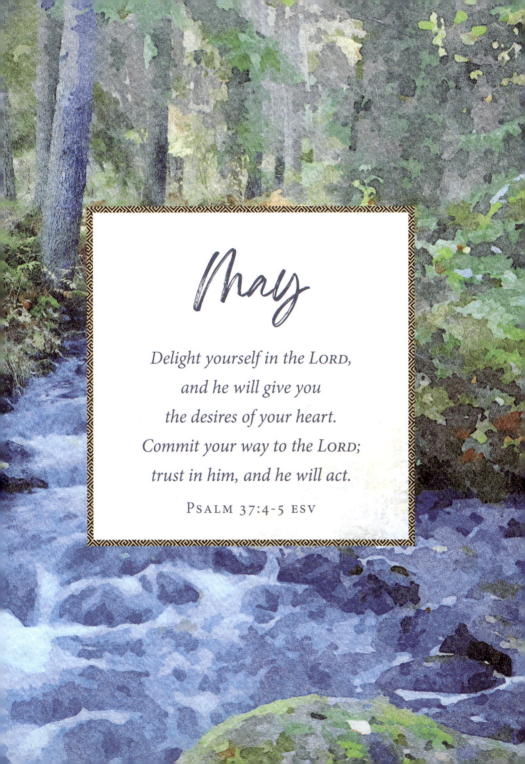

May

Delight yourself in the Lord,
*and he will give you
the desires of your heart.
Commit your way to the* Lord;
trust in him, and he will act.

Psalm 37:4-5 esv

Hard Pressed

When hard pressed, I cried to the LORD;
he brought me into a spacious place.
PSALM 118:5 NIV

You have probably experienced stepping into an elevator with a lot of people in it. When that door closes, it squeezes you in with nowhere to go until the elevator stops and the door opens.

There are a lot of life situations that make you feel pressed in. You might have a deadline looming, too many commitments, or be suffering from financial pressure. When it starts to feel like you are hard pressed, cry out to the Lord. Imagine yourself being stuck in a small room and then see Jesus as he opens the door wide into the big, fresh outdoors. What a relief!

Jesus, I am feeling a bit trapped by my circumstances right now. Please help me find my way out of the situation and bring me into a spacious place where I can breathe freely and think clearly.

Endurance

Wait for the LORD;
be strong and take heart and wait for the LORD.
PSALM 27:14 NIV

Wait for the Lord; wait for the Lord! The Scripture uses this phrase twice in one short sentence, so it must be an important one to think about. Our lives are full of hurry from the moment we wake up to when we lie down. We rush to get ready for work, we rush to get the kids where they need to go, we rush to get to our appointments and fit in all the extra jobs in between.

All of our rushing can mean that we are impatient when it comes to making decisions about important life choices. Instead of rushing to get an answer, allow yourself to stop and wait. Wait for the Lord; he has the best things to share with you, but you will have to stop first to listen.

Lord, I have so much to do every day that I often neglect to wait for your wisdom and guidance. I choose to stop in this moment and wait to hear your voice.

Create and Renew

Create in me a clean heart, O God,
and renew a right spirit within me.
PSALM 51:10 ESV

Springtime is a great time to clear out the clutter and give your home a good onceover. It feels good to be able to sift through everything you've been hanging on to and get rid of the things that aren't working for you anymore. That pile of things to be donated shows the progress you've made.

In the same way that our homes need to be cleared of all the useless items we collect over the years, our souls can use a good refreshing too. Over the years we collect bad habits, wrongful ways of thinking, and relics of our old lifestyles—ones that no longer fit our lives. It's good to examine our hearts and clean out the junk.

Lord, I need you to clear out the junk in my heart. As I launch into my day, remind me of your goodness. Remind me that I need to prioritize things of eternity, not the passing things of today.

The Greatest Drama

Come and see what God has done,
his awesome deeds for mankind!
PSALM 66:5 NIV

Many times in the Psalms, the author's inspiration comes from looking back at the stories of old, recalling with joy how their people were able to overcome hardship and be released into a place of freedom. It is the Lord that has sustained and directed these stories. The author credits the Lord, and calls people to come and witness what he has done.

Do you have stories from your family of God's goodness? Perhaps you are in the middle of making your own story that will be told for generations to come. Be encouraged in your hardship. God will bring something good out of it!

Lord, I am afraid to go through hard times. I don't want to be tested or tried. Thank you for reminding me of the stories of your people who eventually could say that you had done awesome things.

Guard It

Take control of what I say, O Lord,
and guard my lips.
PSALM 141:3 NIV

Have you ever found yourself drawn in to a negative conversation about someone else? You might not have started the conversation but as it goes on you realize that you are contributing more than is wise to. Be encouraged to address those moments and not let them slip by. It's important that we don't compromise our integrity, not because we should feel obligated to do the right thing, but because we want the love of Christ to always be front and center of our conversations and attitudes.

Your mouth can bring harm but it can also bring an incredible amount of good, so be encouraged to bless others through your words.

Lord, I am sorry for the times when I have involved myself in conversations that are unkind toward other people. Help me to let your love come before anything I say.

Highs and Lows

A song. A psalm of David.
My heart is confident in you, O God;
no wonder I can sing your praises with all my heart!
PSALM 108:1 NLT

The Psalms communicate the highs and lows of life, or the mountaintops and valleys. This psalm is a mountaintop moment. David's heart is steadfast.

These are the moments when you feel self-assured, confident of what lies ahead and optimistic for the future; you almost boast about it! Embrace these moments and celebrate with enthusiasm. If you can't celebrate for yourself today, celebrate for someone else.

Father, thank you that I can be confident in you when I'm not confident in myself. Help me to see my worth from your perspective today.

Hear Me

LORD, *hear my prayer,*
listen to my cry for mercy;
in your faithfulness and righteousness
come to my relief.
PSALM 143:1 NIV

Do you think David needed to ask the Lord to hear his prayer? This kind of plea resonates with our humanness; it assures us that it's okay to feel like you need to get God's attention. But even in David's request, he establishes the Lord's faithfulness and righteousness. We are shown here that our prayers and petitions go hand and hand with our humble recognition that our human condition can only be met by a faithful and righteous God. Taking this view puts our needs in perspective and sidelines our ambition.

If you are struggling with understanding a situation, or you're trying to adjust to change or impending decisions, allow yourself to surrender to God's mercy. This is the only thing that will bring you peace.

Faithful God, I am so grateful that you are the true answer to all my needs. Thank you for your faithfulness and righteousness.

Changes

The enemy has pursued me,
crushing me to the ground,
making me live in darkness
like those long dead.
PSALM 143:3 CSB

The reality is that change makes us vulnerable. It can be changes in our financial situation, our family life, or a new house or job. There are risks and pitfalls with each new change. It is, however, inevitable. The universe is in motion and time is a thief.

In moments of risk and uncertainty, doubt, fear, and anxiety flourish. The Psalmist describes these feelings as crushing darkness. The weakness of the human condition, good yet fallen, succumbs to this ever-increasing pressure. How relieving it is that we can ask for help and pray for mercy to a God who listens.

Holy Spirit, I need your power to surge through me in this moment. I feel weak and despairing and very vulnerable. Give me a heavenly perspective that all will be well and that this is momentary.

Stretched Out

I stretch out my hands to you;
my soul thirsts for you like a parched land.
PSALM 143:6 ESV

David takes his eyes off his own situation and reflects on the bigger picture. His desire for relief changes to a desire for connection. The temporary external factors momentarily melt away and eternal relationship takes priority.

This is a powerful reminder of a personal God: a God whose first priority is our relational well-being. This is a hard pill to swallow at times, especially if we are suffering. Faith can feel foolish in certain moments. But David says, "I spread out my hands to you," asking God to make sense and meaning out of his circumstances.

God, help me to be aware of your love for me. I want to feel your fatherly embrace and know you are holding me through my pain and frustration.

Come Quickly

Come quickly, Lord, and answer me,
for my depression deepens.
Don't turn away from me, or I will die.
PSALM 143:7 NLT

The psalmist describes how he is at breaking point, ready to give it up. He prays for the dawn to bring good news, fresh revelation. Control lies with others not with the Psalmist, yet there is still hope, a foundation of trust. What does the unbeliever have to say in these moments of human anguish?

David's faith seeks direction; he asks to be taught and declares trust. Some hardship brings hope and it surely brings wisdom. David trusts that God is in the process. Be encouraged that ultimately God is in control and you can learn to trust him in your process as David did.

Lord, as the world becomes more exposed to issues facing our mental health, don't turn from us. Rescue me from the pressures that make me despair and turn inward. Give me unwavering strength today.

Firmer Ground

Teach me to do your will,
for you are my God.
May your gracious Spirit lead me forward
on a firm footing.
PSALM 143:10 NLT

In a sense David has given up, or, rather, he has surrendered his life. He no longer wishes to fulfil his own desire, his own ambition. The cry of his heart is to walk in complete obedience to God. That is where he is safest. That is where he is most loved and most sure of himself and his destiny.

Again and again in this prayer he affirms God's goodness. Not in an attempt to win God's favor, but as an outpouring of revelation. He has recalled the days long ago; he has understood his suffering and heart focus on God's faithfulness and goodness.

Holy Spirit, lead me today and always, according to your will, not my own.

Not Even One

All have turned away,
all have become corrupt;
there is no one who does good,
not even one.
PSALM 14:3 NIV

Not even one? It sounds like humanity had no hope of doing good! This is the reason for our rescue through Jesus.

When Jesus died on the cross and rose again, he not only took the penalty for our sin, but he became the way in which we can approach God boldly because Jesus made us holy. You are made good, so walk in goodness today.

Jesus, thank you so much for suffering the cross so that I could be completely saved and made holy before God.

Silence Them

Since I am your loving servant,
destroy all those who are trying to harm me.
And because you are so loving and kind to me,
silence all of my enemies!

PSALM 143:12 TPT

When you watch an interesting film about overcoming adversity or a struggle for freedom from oppression, does it inspire you to live a life that is meaningful or to join the cause and be on the right side of good?

Overcoming oppression brings God glory because God is for freedom. David seeks what God seeks (good paths that are pleasing to God) despite the fact that David's enemies sought to destroy him. Life is not neutral; we are either overcoming adversity or we are creating it!

Lord, help me to be slower to anger, richer in love, more faithful, more trusting, and more obedient.

Prayer Answered

O Lord my God, I cried to you for help,
and you have healed me.
Psalm 30:2 esv

The ancient people used the word healing to mean more than just an answer to a physical problem. Pain extends beyond our body's bruises, illness, and disease. We experience pain on an emotional, mental, and sometimes even spiritual level.

All of these discomforts cause us to cry out for help—it is mostly in our distress that we are led toward a plea to be rescued from it. What kind of pain are you facing today? Have confidence in this Scripture that assures us that we will be healed.

Lord, I cry out to you for help. I bring my pain before you and trust that you will bring complete healing. I know that sometimes we don't receive immediate healing, so help me to trust in your lifelong and complete healing.

Busy Busy

"Be still, and know that I am God;
I will be exalted among the nations,
I will be exalted in the earth."
PSALM 46:10 NIV

When we read or watch the news about politics, it can be confusing to understand where and if God's ways ever influence the people who govern our country. We can get busy worrying about all manner of things in our society. The trouble is, when we get consumed with our own opinions, we forget to stop and gain perspective.

This Psalm isn't just asking us to stop and trust; it's asking us to still ourselves from our own busy ways of trying to fix things beyond our understanding, and to know that God is, and always will be, the God who governs this entire universe. Be still in that knowledge as you walk into your day.

Great and mighty God, I am reminded of your unfailing presence and governance of not only this world, but also the entire universe. Help me to put the day-to-day in perspective as I reflect on this truth.

Humility

The lowly will possess the land
and will live in peace and prosperity.
PSALM 37:11 NLT

Our world is really upside down in comparison to God's kingdom. In this life, those who have a lot are able to acquire more. Those who possess the land, or a home on the land, are the wealthy ones. What is this promise that the lowly will possess the land? This is what it looks like in God's kingdom. He values those who are humble; he cares for those in poverty.

This is God's heart. He longs for those who are struggling to come to peace and prosperity. What a beautiful God who watches over us. Instead of worrying about your circumstance, pray for those who are impoverished, that they would live in peace and be blessed.

Beautiful God, I turn my thoughts toward those people who don't have many earthly possessions or are struggling with oppression. Bring freedom and peace to their hearts; bring them prosperity so they can also possess the land.

Weaned

I have calmed and quieted my soul,
like a weaned child with its mother,
like a weaned child is my soul within me.
PSALM 131:2 ESV

One almost wonders if this Psalm was written while the child was sitting with the author. Have you ever had a fussy child finally calm down, relax, and fall asleep on you? It's one of the best feelings in the world to know that the child is now at peace.

This is how the Holy Spirit longs for you to feel. He wants you to stop fussing, to calm down, and to gently rest. Even though this day is about to start and will get busier as you go along, this moment right now is a time to be calm and quiet.

Holy Spirit, thank you for bringing me the comfort that I need so I am no longer striving and stressing about my safety or provision. Thank you for taking care of me today and every day.

Peace Promise

I will listen to what God the LORD says;
he promises peace to his people,
his faithful servants—but let them not turn to folly.
PSALM 85:8 NIV

Fighting when you were young was a little more obvious and matter of fact. If you didn't want to listen to someone, you would say "I'm not listening!" and cover your ears. As we mature, we stop saying the words and covering our ears, but we can still be very defiant and choose not to listen to what others have to say.

Often when we really want something, wisdom might speak to us through God or others, and we turn our backs on that gentle voice. Don't cover your ears today. Listen to the Lord because he brings peace. Not listening to him will only bring you folly.

Jesus, I want to listen to you today. Speak to me; let me clearly hear your voice, and then give me the strength to act with wisdom.

Know It All

You perceive every movement of my heart and soul,
and you understand my every thought
before it even enters my mind.
PSALM 139:2 TPT

You are a complex and beautiful human being. That's because a complex and beautiful God made you! This is why he knows your every movement and understands your personality and the way you think.

God knows the reasons why you make the decisions you make even if you sometimes don't understand them yourself. As you head into the big wide world, know that you are stepping into a day's journey with the person who understands you most at your side.

Jesus, I am so happy to have you as a companion in my day-to-day life. I love that you understand me, and that you understand how I think. Help me to understand more about you too.

Hiding

Where can I go from your Spirit?
Where can I flee from your presence?
PSALM 139:7 NIV

These words were probably very similar to the ones Adam and Eve used in the garden when they were ashamed of their disobedience. It's how we feel when we are ashamed of something that we have done wrong. We want to hide and we don't want to be found!

It's okay to feel bad about doing the wrong thing and to feel guilty about making a wrong decision. But you can't live in that guilt and you can't hide forever. God already knows where you are. He is seeking restoration with you. His Spirit is already with you. If you are trying to run from him it's a losing battle! Instead, surrender to him and let his grace bring you joy.

Lord, I'm sorry for some of the poor choices I have made lately; I am ashamed about some of the things that I have said and done. But I know that I can't run from you, so instead I choose to run to you.

Only Light

There is no such thing as darkness with you.
The night, to you, is as bright as the day;
there's no difference between the two.
PSALM 139:12 TPT

During the summer months, the North Pole experiences twenty-four hours of daylight each day! Some countries in the northern hemisphere don't get dark until midnight or beyond. This is because of the relationship and position to the sun: the source of light.

Imagine God, then, who is nothing but light! Everywhere he goes he brings light, and he doesn't see or experience darkness the way you do. It's a mind-blowing thought, and even more interesting if you think about it metaphorically. God is not bothered, put off, or disoriented in the dark, because he simply doesn't experience it as darkness. Wrap your head around that today!

Heavenly Father, I am in awe of how great and wonderful you are. Help me to understand you and your ways in a completely different light today.

Offended

See if there is any offensive way in me
and lead me in the way everlasting.
PSALM 139:24 NIV

Have you taken any personality tests, or tried to figure out what type of person you are? We all know people who are the type to speak their minds even if the words come out offensively. Perhaps you are one of those people! Even if you aren't intentionally trying to cause offense, unfiltered thoughts that land as words can end up being hurtful. If this is one of your vices, take an extra second to think before you speak. It can help to switch that filter on that tells you when you are about to say something rude or unkind.

In the same way, if you are prone to being offended, take a look at the heart of the person who said the wrong thing. Were they really trying to hurt you? Offense is hard, whether you are on the giving or receiving end of it, so allow God's grace to enter those situations.

God help me in my offense whether I am giving or receiving it. I want to be loving and filled with grace for others. I need you to show me how.

Keep Me Safe

Keep me safe, my God,
for in you I take refuge.
PSALM 16:1 NIV

What are the things that make you feel the most safe? Is it knowing that you can go for a walk outside without worrying? Is it feeling like your home is a place of rest? Depending on where you live and what your home situation is like, your idea of safety is wrapped up in feeling like no one will bring you harm.

We have a strong survival instinct and will do what is best to keep us from being hurt, physically and emotionally. God is a person who will always be safe. He does not harm you and will never hurt you in any way. Take refuge in a God who is completely on your side.

Thank you, God, that you are my defender and protector. You are the best place for me to run when I am in need of safety and assurance. Help me to seek you out before I look to other things to fill that need in me.

Make Haste

Hurry to help me,
my Lord, my salvation.
PSALM 38:22 CSB

When we are in a rush or feeling pressured, sometimes the only thing we can speak, or maybe even think is, "help." This morning might be the first time you have stopped for a few minutes in an otherwise rushed start to the day. God doesn't need you to come up with lengthy prayers to explain where you are at. If you just feel like you need some help, ask him!

The cry in this Scripture is for God to help quickly, and we are allowed to ask God for that. With a God who is so near, a prayer to ask for his presence is immediate! He's here with you right now, ready to save you.

Make haste to help me, O Lord, my salvation! You are always ready to come to my aid and I am so grateful for that.

Soul Keeper

The LORD will protect you from all evil;
He will keep your soul.
PSALM 121:7 NASB

It might be hard to reconcile this verse to your life experience because bad things do happen, and they happen to all kinds of people. God's protection, however, goes a lot deeper than we understand. Your soul—the thing that make you uniquely you—is guarded and fully protected by the one true living God. He created you, and he will keep you!

Even when troubles come knocking at your door, they cannot rob you of your soul. This morning, find your peace with this world, knowing that you are kept safely in God's hands.

Jesus, I am glad to have a new perspective on what it means to be protected from evil. Thank you that there is no one like me, and that is exactly how you intended it to be! I am made by you and therefore kept by you.

Coming and Going

The LORD keeps watch over you as you come and go,
both now and forever.
PSALM 121:8 NLT

When you leave the house, picture an adoring parent watching a child leave for school. Picture them blowing you a kiss, waving goodbye, and making sure you get safely to the bus or cross walk. Their loving eye is always on you.

This is how the Lord watches you. He adores you so much that he watches carefully, making sure you are okay! His gaze doesn't stop at the front door, he will be with you throughout your entire day.

Lord, thank you for the care and concern you have for me. Let me remember that your loving gaze is on me the whole day.

Simple

The LORD preserves the simple;
when I was brought low, he saved me.
PSALM 116:6 ESV

It doesn't feel that nice to be called simple, but we are all a little inexperienced, helpless, and even foolish at times. We make decisions simply because we want to do something, not necessarily because it is the smartest thing to do.

Don't worry; God knows that his creation can be a lot like sheep, and he watches over us anyway. If you make a mistake today, pick yourself up and let God help you brush off the dirt. You will be okay.

Thanks, good God, for watching over me even when I do stupid things. I am sorry that I often put myself before others. Teach me your ways, so I become more wise.

Peacemaker

Consider the blameless, observe the upright;
a future awaits those who seek peace.
PSALM 37:37 NIV

Peaceful ways give birth to righteousness. There are times when conflict cannot be avoided, but assuming the role of the peacemaker is often far better than getting your own way. To be a peacemaker requires humility and the desire for the greater good.

Whatever environment you are going to be in today, remember the importance of being someone who seeks to do the right thing by everyone.

God, your Word says that you are the author of peace. Bring peace to my situations, peace in my decisions, and peace in my heart. Help me to become a peacemaker today so the fruit that I bear in my life will be that of righteousness.

Magnificent

What honor you have given to men,
created only a little lower than Elohim,
crowned like kings and queens
with glory and magnificence.

PSALM 8:5 TPT

On the sixth day, after all other created things, God made man and woman. He made us in his image; this Scripture compares us to kings and queens! On that day he declared that his creation was very good.

How reassuring it is to know that God's creation was intentionally good. He did not create us with mistakes or flaws; he created us according to his perfect plan. As you wake up to a new day, consider how magnificent humanity is, and with that, how magnificent you are!

Thank you, God, for your very good creation. Help me to see beyond this life to the life to come where you will restore your creation to your perfect will.

No More Tears

For you have delivered my soul from death,
my eyes from tears, my feet from stumbling.
PSALM 116:8 ESV

We are promised a time where there will be no more death, tears, or stumbling. This life is full of hardships, but we can live in hope that a day will come where joy will reign supreme. It is this hope that carries us through the hard times when we trust that God is still good and that he has good plans for us now and especially in the life to come.

Try to bravely face this day with joy concerning your future. This is not where it ends!

Lord, I look forward to an eternity of joy, where the pain of this life will be no more. Thank you that even today you can bring relief to my physical pain, healing to my emotional pain, and restoration to my spiritual weakness. Help me to lean on you through the hard times and give me strength to live with eternity in mind.

Family and Friends

For the sake of my family and friends, I will say,
"Peace be within you."
PSALM 122:8 NIV

Family members can be some of the hardest people to get along with at times. In the same way, people within our church or community of believers are not always easy to show love to. Often it is more difficult to keep the peace between families than a group of strangers.

For the sake of your family and friends, it's important to approach a situation with the intention of keeping love at the center. Remember that in your conversations today.

I am blessed, Jesus, to have close friends and family in my life. Teach me to be aware of the times when I am being confrontational or unnecessarily disagreeable. Help me to strive for peace.

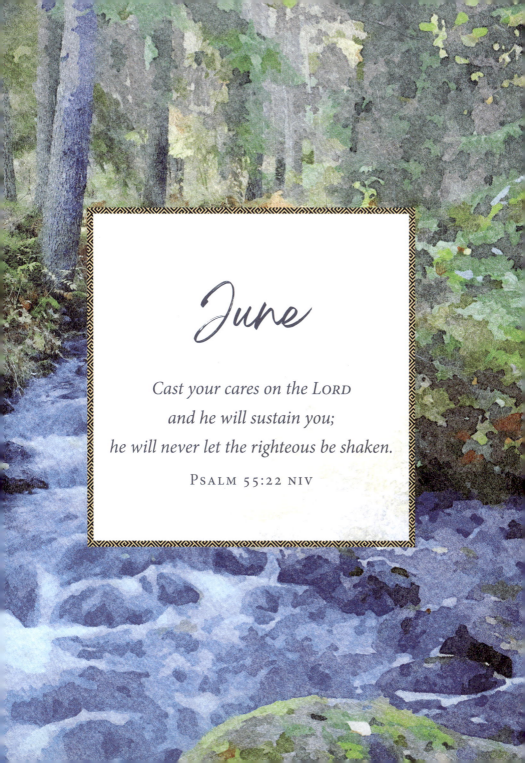

June

*Cast your cares on the L*ORD
and he will sustain you;
he will never let the righteous be shaken.

PSALM 55:22 NIV

So Pretty

Praise him, sun and moon,
praise him, all you shining stars!
PSALM 148:3 ESV

It is amazing enough that the Lord made the earth and everything in it, from the blade of grass to the complexities of conception. Even more amazing is that he created the heavens, the universe, and everything beyond that.

In their own way, all of these living things praise the Lord. The sun reflects his glory, the moon his mystery, and the stars his infinite being. As you rise with the sun this morning, think of your own way to honor your Creator.

Heavenly Creator, I am in awe of everything you have made. I want to praise you in whatever way I can. Help me to be a reflection of you in some way today.

Surround Me

You, O Lord, are a shield about me,
my glory, and the lifter of my head.
PSALM 3:3 ESV

Today may you be reminded that God is your comforter. That he does not leave you nor forsake you. That whatever is before you, he sees it and he protects you as a shield protects a warrior. He lifts your head when you want to put it down. He tells you to look up and see his smile shining down on you. He will never let you go and will never let you fall apart.

Whatever is before you, know who is walking beside you holding your hand. As you step in faith, know who is lighting your path. As you cry, know who lifts your head. What a father he is.

God, thank you for protecting me, for sending your Son to die for me so I can be free. Thank you for always walking with me and seeing me as I am.

Unqualified

Though a mighty army surrounds me,
my heart will not be afraid.
Even if I am attacked,
I will remain confident.
PSALM 27:3 NLT

Whether bringing a brand new baby home from the hospital, giving your first major presentation at work, or simply making your first Thanksgiving meal, there's probably been at least one moment in your life that had you thinking, I have no idea what I'm doing. I'm not qualified.

What did you do? You probably had little option but to dive on in! Let your confidence in God's ability be the driver today. You can feel a lot calmer when you realize this day does not have to be done in your own strength.

Lord, I give you my day, knowing that you are qualified enough to make it a great one. Help me to remember that I am not alone.

Serenity

He makes peace in your borders;
he fills you with the finest of the wheat.
PSALM 147:14 ESV

I can't get a moment's peace. Sound familiar? We all go through seasons where it seems every corner hides a new challenge to our serenity, assuming we've actually achieved any semblance of serenity in the first place. Why is it so hard to find peace in this world? Because we're looking in this world.

True peace is found in Jesus. There will be a lot of things that try to take away your sense of peace today, but if you allow the Holy Spirit to speak to you, your day will be filled with moments of knowing that he is near.

Lord, let your words of life bring peace to my heart throughout my day.

From the Source

*Do not cast me away from Your presence
And do not take Your Holy Spirit from me.*
PSALM 51:11 NASB

The best way to know if something is true, or right, is to hear it for yourself—straight from the source. You believe you nailed the interview, but you don't believe you got the job until you get the phone call. You feel you might be pregnant, but you wait for the test results before telling anyone.

What about God? How can you hear from him? How do you discern his will for your life? Think about the voices that come into your life today and remember to keep his voice at the forefront.

Father God, thank you that you can speak to me through your Word and through your Holy Spirit. Guide me in your righteousness this day.

Bit and Bridle

Do not be like a senseless horse or mule
that needs a bit and bridle
to keep it under control.
PSALM 32:9 NLT

Do you ever feel like you are not being heard? It can be frustrating and discouraging when you realize the person you are talking to is not really listening.

Are you willing to tune in to what others are saying today? It may be a gentle rebuke, some great advice, or an encouraging word. Whatever it is, allow God's grace in your conversations, and humbly listen to what he wants you to hear.

Lord, help me to take the time to listen to others today. Help me to try to understand the heart of the matter and give me the grace to keep the peace.

Empty Breath

The Lord knows our thoughts,
that they are but an empty breath.
PSALM 94:11 NRSV

Do you ever catch yourself dwelling on the negative aspects of life? We can be nonchalant when someone tells us good news, but talk for hours about conflict, worries, and disappointment. It is good to communicate things that aren't going so well in our lives, but we can also fall into the trap of setting our minds on the wrong things.

Give your mind over to truth and honor, pure and lovely things today. You are sure to find goodness in unexpected places!

God, thank you for creating me with your goodness in my heart. If I am tempted today with negative talk or harmful gossip, I pray you would give me the wisdom and grace to resist the bad and choose good.

Aching Bones

Have mercy on me, Lord, for I am faint;
heal me, Lord, for my bones are in agony.
PSALM 6:2 NIV

Did you have trouble getting up this morning? Maybe it was too dark, you had a late night, or your bones were too achy to want to move! Our lifestyle doesn't allow us to just stay in bed as long as we need to, there are kids, jobs, or classes to attend to and those things don't wait for you.

We are prone to staying up too late, forgetting to eat breakfast, and generally just rushing around a lot. This can make us faint and tired by the end of the day. Ask the Lord for energy, and then make some wise choices about your schedule so you can endure the day ahead.

Lord, have mercy on me. I am feeling tired and sore, and I need to last through the day. Give me the wisdom to do the healthiest things for my body and mind.

Which Road

Show me the right path, O Lord;
point out the road for me to follow.
PSALM 25:4 NLT

It is hard to get lost with our digital maps to guide us every step of the way. You type in an address and start driving, leaving the rest up to the voice on your phone. When it comes to making decisions in your everyday life, do you expect God to speak directly and specifically to you? Do you get disorientated when you don't hear straight away?

God doesn't always answer instantly or in the way that might you expect, but you can trust that he will show you the right path. Be encouraged if you are in the middle of a confusing situation, to wait and listen for the road that he is pointing you toward.

Show me, Lord, which path to take. When I am at the crossroads, I need you to give me some clear direction. I humbly accept that your way is better than mine.

Let's Chat

My heart has heard you say,
"Come and talk with me."
And my heart responds,
"LORD, I am coming."
PSALM 27:8 NLT

Isn't it a blessing to be able to catch up with friends and family over coffee or a phone call? You might have those kinds of plans today, where you intend on having a conversation and share with someone what has been going on in your life.

Isn't it beautiful that God is inviting you into this kind of conversation with him? Listen to your heart for a moment and hear him say, "Come and talk with me!" Make a point of having some time with him. Sit down, walk, talk, and listen. Your heart will be full after engaging in a loving conversation with your friend.

Thank you, Lord, for the opportunity to come and talk with you. I want to make time for you right now, or sometime today, where we can share with each other.

Glory Garments

Honor the LORD for the glory of his name.
Worship the LORD in the splendor of his holiness.
PSALM 29:2 NLT

OMG. It's a common e-phrase we throw around and you may have various opinions about using it as an expression. Whatever your thoughts, it proves a point that we use God's name a lot and often with very little respect or reverence. The Jewish tradition considers the name of God to be so sacred that it is substituted with Adonai, meaning my Lord.

There are hundreds of names used in Scripture for God, and what we can be certain of is that we want to honor and worship the God who is our personal Creator and who is so present with us. Give him that honor today.

Adonai, you are worthy of my praise. You are worthy of the world's praise, and I am grieved that people don't know you yet. Show your glory and use me to share it.

Wailing to Whirling

You have turned my mourning into joyful dancing.
You have taken away my clothes of mourning
and clothed me with joy.
PSALM 30:11 NLT

Have you experienced driving through a really long tunnel and only knowing that there was an end because of the number markings on the wall or your GPS telling you it was coming to an end? If you didn't have any idea, those tunnels could seem really long and a little bit scary.

Grief and heartache can sometimes feel like an endless tunnel with little to tell you how long or how much more you will have to endure. If this is you right now, find courage in the psalm above—of one who has found the joy and light at the end of their tunnel. It does happen, and it will happen for you. Your mourning will one day turn to joy.

Jesus, I choose to be strengthened by the hope that my mourning can be turned to joy. I will keep trusting you while I am in the middle of it.

Out of the Pit

You brought me up from the grave, O Lord.
You kept me from falling into the pit of death.
PSALM 30:3 NLT

It is hard to understand how and when God heals his children. Have you prayed for healing recently and haven't got any better? Do you know someone around you that is unwell and not recovering?

It can be disheartening when you are sick or see others that you care about not improving. Our faith does not need to be great, but through our belief in Jesus we can also acknowledge our belief in the miracles that he performed. Jesus showed us that what we think is impossible is not impossible with God.

Jesus, I pray for healing in my life and in the life of those who are unwell around me. I know that you cared for others and that you had compassion to heal, but I also recognize that sometimes you don't answer us exactly how we want. Help me to trust that you are always good, no matter what.

He Knows

I will rejoice and be glad in Your faithfulness,
Because You have seen my misery;
You have known the troubles of my soul.
PSALM 31:7 NASB

Do you ever sit down to pray and find yourself struggling to find the words to begin? You stumble over your words; your mind draws a blank. You want to be obedient by spending time with the Lord, but you don't even know where to begin.

When you find yourself searching for the right way to express what you want to say to God, know that he will intercede if you allow him to. Spend some time sitting quietly and let him take the reins for you today. He knows the troubles of your soul.

Lord, I don't always know what to pray, so I ask that right now you would take over. You know my heart and my needs, and even my wants. I pray for your will to be done.

Out of Sight

Oh, what joy for those whose disobedience is forgiven,
whose sin is put out of sight!
PSALM 32:1 NLT

Is your heart feeling a little heavy this morning because of something that just isn't sitting right about what you said or did to someone else? Maybe you are feeling upset about something that was said or done to you.

You have a mediator in Christ, who can cover matters of your own sin, and help you heal when you have been wronged. Let him help you through it so you can reach the place of freedom and joy.

Thank you, Jesus, for helping me to overcome my sin. Thank you for showing me that my sin is put out of sight!

Come Clean

Many are the sorrows of the wicked,
but steadfast love surrounds the one
who trusts in the LORD.
PSALM 32:10 ESV

God provides us relief from any bondage we carry. Our Father can take any mistake we've made in the past and release the beauty in that error.

We don't need to be so hard on ourselves. We don't need to feel trapped, or think we've failed, or hold on so tightly that we can't see the joy in our current circumstance.

Jesus, thank you for your forgiveness. Thank you that you keep cheering me on even when I stumble. Be gracious to me today, so I can persevere in all that you have laid before me. Help me to have the end destination in mind.

Justice

He loves righteousness and justice;
the earth is full of the steadfast love of the Lord.
PSALM 33:5 ESV

There are few things worse than being unjustly wronged. It's not easy when you are hurt—especially by someone close to you. A deep part of each of us cries out for justice. It's a God-given trait, meant to call us to stand in the gap for the hurting, the widow, the orphan—it's our longing for true religion.

When we identify injustice, that longing rises up strongly. We feel pain, hurt, confusion, and pressure. And more than all of those emotions, we feel the deep need to see justice served. Justice isn't your responsibility, so let go and trust that love and truth will prevail.

God, give me the grace today to forgive those who have wronged me. Forgive those who are hurting others. I am overwhelmed by injustice, so I pray for your righteousness to prevail.

Forever Firm

The plans of the LORD stand firm forever,
the purposes of his heart through all generations.
PSALM 33:11 NIV

We live in an ever-changing world where nothing stays the same for very long. Just when you thought you had everything working for you, something changes and it can set off a string of other changes. This can be unsettling because we like to be comfortable. The hardest part, yet most wonderful thing, about getting uncomfortable is that it provides an environment for personal growth.

If change is coming your way, remember that you are invited into a process that, if you allow it, will mature and strengthen you. The best thing about all your changes is that you can be assured that God's plans are firm and they are forever. You are loved, you will be taken care of, and eternity is part of your future.

Lord, in those times I feel unsettled because of all the changes, remind me that the purpose of your heart has lasted throughout the generations.

JUNE 19

War Horse

The war horse is a false hope for salvation,
and by its great might it cannot rescue.
PSALM 33:17 ESV

It's unfortunate that part of the human condition is to try and win things through force. There is always a part of the world that remains in conflict over religion, resources, and territory. On a smaller scale, our personal battles are often fought with manipulation and with the goal to win. But arguments are never won, they only create more heat and resentment. We can't save ourselves, or a situation, through competition.

If you are in the middle of a struggle right now, remember what salvation is really all about. It's a gift that none of us fought for or won: a gift from Jesus and through Jesus. Accept that gift and offer a gift of grace in the middle of your difficulties.

Jesus, I am sorry when I have tried to win a fight through argument or stubbornness. I am reminded of your amazing grace that saved me. Save my relationships through this same grace.

Let It Out

When I refused to confess my sin,
my body wasted away,
and I groaned all day long.
PSALM 32:3 NLT

You might be able to relate all too well to this psalm. The problem with keeping sin inside is that you never become free from it. But let's reframe the idea of sin for just a minute. It's not just a list of bad things that you shouldn't do. Sin is focusing so much on yourself that you separate yourself from God.

Anything that takes your eyes of Jesus can eat away at you when you keep it to yourself. Release your burden of "sin"; share your heart with Jesus and free yourself from the relentless pain of holding on to something that isn't good for you.

Jesus, I need your grace. I don't want to keep anything else inside, so I release all those things that I have been storing up on the inside and pray that you would grant me freedom.

Befriend Faithfulness

Trust in the LORD, and do good;
dwell in the land and befriend faithfulness.
PSALM 37:3 ESV

Our lives can feel unpredictable, illogical, and inconsistent at times. Changes in work, marriage, family, or church can make the road seem irrational, uneven, and confusing. God makes us the promise of a steadfast path when we keep his covenant.

When we consider our lives through our limited human perspective, the path seems wavering. But the guidance of Jesus Christ is, in fact, steadfast.

Lord, thank you for all the wonderful promises that you have made for me. Help me to keep my end of the promise too, and continue to be faithful to you. I choose to walk in your ways today.

Staying Put

There's no doubt about it;
God holds our lives safely in his hands.
He's the one who keeps us faithfully following him.
PSALM 66:9 TPT

When riding in a moving car, boat, or plane, we wouldn't just jump out, no matter how restless or impatient we were feeling. That would be crazy. We couldn't possibly expect to arrive at our destination as safely or as quickly—or perhaps at all.

We grasp the necessity of remaining where we are if we are to get where we are going. Why are we so quick to jump ahead when it comes to God's plans for our lives? Spend some time praying for the Spirit to reveal to you anywhere you are not abiding in Jesus or trusting his timing. Ask him to help you trust him.

Jesus, I want to remain in you by staying close by your side as we walk this journey together. Help me to trust that you are bringing me with you and not leaving me alone.

Settled

There your people finally settled,
and with a bountiful harvest, O God,
you provided for your needy people.
PSALM 68:10 NLT

There are seasons in our lives where we feel restless and unsettled. You may want to move on from your job, get out of the neighborhood you are in, or perhaps you are just anxious to start a new chapter of your life. Sometimes there is nothing to define your restlessness; you just know you feel unsettled.

God knows that people long to feel comfortable, at peace, and settled. This is why he brought the Israelites out of slavery and into a place they could finally call home. If you are in a season of unsettledness, ask God to provide a place for you to go.

Lord, there are times when I just want to move on. I don't like where I am and I feel restless. In these times, please give me the ability to be content while I wait for your guidance toward the next thing.

Empty Stares

Their insults have broken my heart,
and I am in despair.
If only one person would show some pity;
if only one would turn and comfort me.
PSALM 69:20 NLT

Sticks and stones may break my bones, but names will never hurt me. It's not true, is it? The raw pain of an insult can almost be worse than a broken bone. You will know what it feels like to be accused of things you haven't done, or even worse, be made to feel ashamed for things that you have done.

You can probably think of a time when you made a mistake and others ungraciously pointed it out. It's such a relief when you find one person who will reach out with grace. Be thankful, today, for those people in your life who you know would be the ones to stand up for you in your times of greatest shame.

God, I am sorry for some of the shameful mistakes I have made. I have felt embarrassed and guilty, yet I know that this isn't the way that you want me to feel. Thank you so much for your grace that releases me from despairing of wrong.

Equality

Help him judge your people in the right way;
let the poor always be treated fairly.
PSALM 72:2 NLT

If you live in a first world country, you might not be confronted with poverty every day. But it is out there. If you visited the streets of downtown, you would see it; if you walked around a poor neighborhood, you would sense it. If you ever had the chance to visit a third world country, you would live it.

Poverty is real and has been since as long as we know. Jesus talked about it at every opportunity. He cared deeply for the less fortunate and asked us to take care of the poor. Let your heart melt for the poor. Be ready to stand up for them and give generously to make sure they are treated well.

Father, I am sorry when I have turned a blind eye to the poverty in this world. I know there are people who have nothing, so I ask you to give me a generous heart toward those who are vulnerable and need help.

Righteous Answers

By awesome deeds you answer us with righteousness,
O God of our salvation,
the hope of all the ends of the earth
and of the farthest seas.
PSALM 65:5 ESV

What have you been asking of God lately? It could be healing from illness, prayer for someone close to you who is hurting, or maybe you just need a little help in your relationships. It is often said that God hears our prayers; yet you might feel like he has never answered yours.

God can seem very far away and unconcerned with your requests and needs. These feelings, however, are not the truth. The truth is that God is always very near to you. He knows your heart, he knows what you need, and he will answer. Trust him as you read this Scripture again and know that he will answer your prayers with amazing wonders and inspiring displays of power. Let this increase your faith today.

O God of my salvation, you are my hope that extends to the ends of the earth and farthest of seas.

Who You Are

Father to the fatherless, defender of widows—
this is God, whose dwelling is holy.
PSALM 68:5 NLT

The amazing thing about our Creator is that he knows who we
need him to be to us in every moment. What kind of person do
you need in your life right now? Is it someone who will accept you
for who you are? Someone to protect you? Is it simply someone to
talk to about your day-to-day life with?

God wants to be that person to you right now. He wants to be a
father figure, a spouse, or a friend. Let him draw near to you this
morning and be the person you need him to be.

Jesus, I need you right now. I need a person I can confide in,
depend on, and even laugh with. Be that to me in this moment.

Cry of Distress

Save me, O God,
for the floodwaters are up to my neck.
PSALM 69:1 NLT

Hopefully you have never had to experience a real flood, but you have probably seen the news when storms or tsunamis hit shores and cause devastation. Metaphorically speaking, it can be distressing when you feel as though you are drowning in chores, childcare, work, or study. Sometimes you feel like you can't get above your emotions and they are crowding you in until you feel like those floodwaters are up to your neck.

Don't give up! This is the time to press into God and ask him to save you. Just because you feel like there is no way out doesn't mean that there isn't. Don't despair; God is right here to give you courage and pull you out of the floodwaters.

O God, I am feeling overwhelmed by everything that I have to do, and it is crowding my mind and emotions. I am up to my neck! Please pull me out of these waters.

Oceans

You rule the raging of the sea;
when its waves rise, you still them.
PSALM 89:9 ESV

If you've ever had the privilege of booking a vacation near the ocean, the most expensive rooms will be the one with ocean views. We love to look at the vastness of the ocean, the deep blue of the waters, and watch the rise and fall of the waves. We might enjoy watching others surf, seeing the skill of how they move across the water.

How different an experience it is when you are in that same water! The waves that crashed so beautifully on the shore are the same waves that dump you on the sand. The sea has a sense of raging, but this is nothing in comparison to the Creator of the waves. Trust in the Creator today.

Beautiful Creator, I am in awe of your creation. I am in awe of the one who created such magnificent things. You are so worthy to be praised.

Whatever Comes

I will be strength to him
and I will give him my grace
to sustain him no matter what comes.
PSALM 89:21 TPT

This verse was God's promise to David when he chose him to be the king of Israel. We have the hindsight to know the mistakes and troubles that David went through. Scripture tells us David's story of blessing, sin, consequence, joy, battles, fear, and love.

David went through a lot in his life and the truth of this verse prevailed. God gave him grace and sustained him no matter what came. Let this verse be your promise today. Trust God to shower you with grace that will sustain you through everything you face today.

Lord, I need your strength for today. Thank you that I can face the day with confidence because I know that you will sustain me.

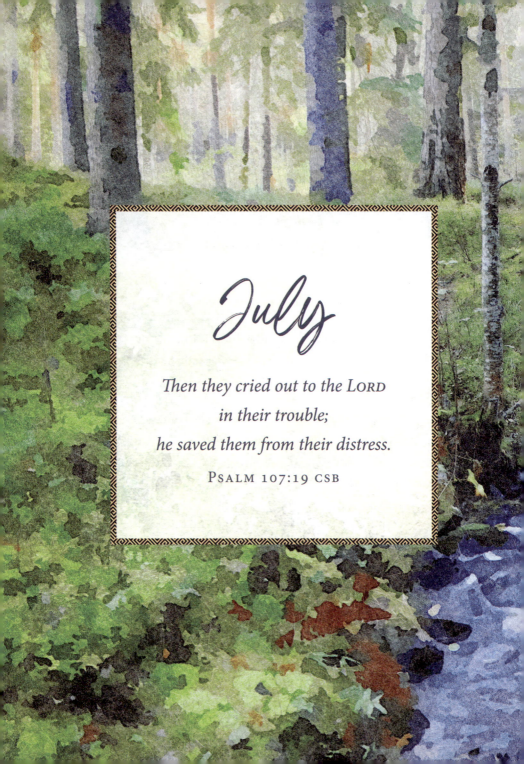

July

Then they cried out to the LORD
in their trouble;
he saved them from their distress.

PSALM 107:19 CSB

Power of Love

Put not your trust in princes,
in a son of man,
in whom there is no salvation.

PSALM 146:3 ESV

When Jesus, the long-awaited Messiah, revealed his deity to his family, disciples, and the crowds, they were expecting a mighty king who would deliver them from their oppressors and establish his everlasting kingdom. What they got was a humble servant who dined with tax collectors and whose feet were cleansed by the tears of a prostitute.

Jesus wasn't exactly what they thought he would be. He was better! Jesus is the good news people have been waiting for.

Jesus, I know that you are good news for me. Help me to proclaim your good news to others. Give me boldness to say why I am full of hope and peace and life. Give me opportunities to share your love.

New Stuff

Praise the LORD!
Sing to the LORD a new song.
Sing his praises in the assembly of the faithful.
PSALM 149:1 NLT

We are obsessed with new things. We like new gadgets, new technology, new clothes, new cars, and new homes. New things represent something fresh, exciting, improved, and enjoyable.

New things are a privilege that not everyone gets to enjoy. Be thankful today for the new things that are in your life. You don't have to feel guilty about your blessings, but make sure you enjoy them and keep them in perspective with what really matters in life.

Lord, I am blessed with many new things. I pray for those less fortunate than me—those who rarely have something new. Help me to become more generous.

Soul Celebration

Let all that I am praise the LORD;
may I never forget the good things he does for me.
PSALM 103:2 NLT

Do you sometimes have those moments of walking into a room and forgetting why you went there in the first place? Our minds are often full of so many things—family, work, church, relationships, chores, and events. Forgetfulness can be a product of not giving yourself time and space to clear your mind and heart. It takes discipline to remind yourself of the good and right things to think about.

Take some time today to focus your soul on Jesus. Try to think of at least one good thing that he has done for you lately. Keep thanking him for that good thing. Make it a habit to bring thankfulness into your prayer time with him.

Jesus, I thank you so much for the good things that you have done for me. My whole being will remember those good things and praise you for them.

Crowned with Love

He redeems me from death
and crowns me with love and tender mercies.
PSALM 103:4 NLT

What a simple and radically beautiful verse of salvation this is! We were all headed for death as a result of trying to live our own ways. Then Jesus came to rescue humanity from death by showing us his way.

The way of Christ is a way of love, mercy, and ultimately a revelation of the new life that he has prepared for us. Enjoy the incredible freedom of knowing that you have been saved and crowned with love.

Jesus, I humbly acknowledge that I can do nothing to save myself. Thank you that I live a life that you have redeemed and are restoring. Lift me up in strength today.

Hyssop

Cleanse me with hyssop, and I will be clean;
wash me, and I will be whiter than snow.
PSALM 51:7 NIV

Hyssop appears in the Bible many times, so it is probably worth a little history lesson. Hyssop was a plant that was prolific in the Middle East and was an herb in the mint family. It was used for cleansing, medicine, and flavor, and God commanded the Israelites to use it in the sacrificial ceremonies.

Hyssop was also used at Jesus' crucifixion to raise the drink of vinegar to his mouth. It could be that this herb was a symbol of the cleansing work that Jesus did on the cross. No longer do you need to confess through ceremonial cleansing, Jesus has made you clean through a simple confession of your mouth.

Jesus, thank you for enduring the cross for me so all my dirt and darkness has been washed away.

A Willing Spirit

*Restore to me the joy of your salvation
and grant me a willing spirit, to sustain me.*
PSALM 51:12 NIV

We could wish all we wanted that we would be perfectly obedient, but we know that we could never measure up to that standard. That's why we ask God to get into the picture and grant us a willing spirit.

Too often, we know the right thing to do, the right words to say, and the right behaviors, but just as often, we don't do the right things, or say the right words, or behave the right way! Let Jesus in today, knowing that you need him to sustain you.

Father, grant me a willing spirit. I want to obey you, yet I know I am prone to wandering and going off course. Keep me on track and right by your side.

Completely Covered

Let all who take refuge in you be glad;
let them ever sing for joy.
Spread your protection over them,
that those who love your name may rejoice in you.
PSALM 5:11 NIV

Consider for a moment the most joyous time of your walk with Christ. Imagine the delight of that season, the lightness and pleasure in your heart. Rest in the memory for a minute, and let the emotions come back to you. Is the joy returning? Do you feel it?

Now, hear this truth: the way you felt about God at the highest, most joyful, amazing, glorious moment is how he feels about you at all times. When you realize how good he is, and that he has granted you everything you need for salvation through Jesus, you can rejoice.

God, you have made me strong. Thank you that I don't have to worry about who I might face today because I have you right next to me, rescuing me from all unrighteousness.

Keep Smiling

Let your shining face shine on me.
Let your undying love and glorious grace
save me from all this gloom.
PSALM 31:16 TPT

Hopefully you will smile a lot throughout your day today. You will probably smile as you greet the people you cross paths with, you might smile as you say goodbye to your loved ones for the day. You might even share a few laughs with friends or the people you work with.

We don't give much thought to a smile, yet it's a really powerful sign that can cheer someone up in an instant. If you haven't gotten any smiles yet today, look to your heavenly Father. Imagine him looking at you and giving you a great big, appreciative and loving smile. You are precious to him.

Thank you, Father, that when I am feeling full of gloom, you are there to lift me up with a smile that tells me I am loved.

Unexpected Strength

Be strong, and let your heart take courage,
all you who wait for the LORD!
PSALM 31:24 ESV

Our lives are full of circumstances that make us feel weak. We are prone to comparisons and sometimes we measure our strength against others. We feel like we are less beautiful, less skilled, less able. But strength isn't always what our human minds are conditioned to think it is.

Remind yourself of Jesus as he carried his own cross, the verbal abuse he took from the crowd, and the pain that he willingly suffered as he was left to die. The acceptance and endurance of pain and the lack of violence and fighting was all a part of Jesus showing courage and strength in an entirely different way than expected. Take courage. You are stronger than you think.

Jesus, thank you for revealing a different kind of strength than the world expects. Help me to accept that I am strong and continue to give me courage.

First Responder

He has not despised or scorned
the suffering of the afflicted one;
he has not hidden his face from him
but has listened to his cry for help.
PSALM 22:24 NIV

Reading or watching the news can leave us feeling pretty hopeless about the state of our world. We see stories of people whose lives have been ruined by injustice, discrimination, war, and natural disasters. The lives of those who are vulnerable to personal destruction need protection, and it needs to come from those of us who are strong enough to help.

God has not hidden his face from these people, and as his image bearers we can be a part of transforming the ugliness of this world into the beauty of his kingdom. What part can you play in helping others today?

God, I want to proudly represent the kind of loving person that you are. Help me not to turn away from those who need help but to listen and respond.

Distressed

Turn to me and have mercy,
for I am alone and in deep distress.
PSALM 25:16 NLT

This time should be a time to feel hopeful about the day ahead, but you might be experiencing just the opposite. If it's dark and you are not looking forward to what you are facing today, you might feel alone and distressed.

Don't let the dread of the day keep you from facing it. You are not alone, even this psalm proves that people have been feeling like this from the ancient days. Cry out to God for deliverance from your feeling of distress and let him work his unexplainable peace into your heart.

Lord, sometimes I can't shake the feeling of stress, anxiety, and just a general feeling of being down and alone. Give me some perspective today and help me to break through the darkness into your light.

Bad Company

I do not spend time with liars,
nor do I make friends with those who hide their sin.
PSALM 26:4 NCV

It's true that you are shaped by who you spend your time with.
If you are a parent, you might have experienced worry over the
friends your child is spending time with because you know that
they have a lot of influence over each other.

We are called to love everyone, but that doesn't mean that we have
to be friends with people who lie and are deceitful. Ultimately
these kinds of relationships will either drag you down or really
hurt you. Take some time today to evaluate who you are hanging
out with and ask God to show you wisdom.

Lord, I know that sometimes I am too influenced by people in my
life who don't follow you. Help me to choose to spend my time
with people who are encouraging, honest, and trustworthy.

Be Sure

Know that the LORD has set apart
his faithful servant for himself;
the LORD hears when I call to him.
PSALM 4:3 NIV

Do you know those people that seem to be confident about everything they say and do? Do you sometimes wish to be as confident as they are? Being confident isn't the same as being prideful or arrogant. It is an inner peace and acceptance of who you are, and it is something that can't be shaken by external opinions or judgements.

This verse exudes confidence, "The Lord hears when I call to him." This confidence can only come from someone who is so sure of how much they are accepted and loved that they know their God will hear them. May this be your confidence today and always.

God, I don't always feel like I am a faithful servant that deserves you to listen to me. Yet, I know that you care so much about me, so give me the confidence to know that you hear me as I pray to you.

The Good Leader

There are many who say,
"Who will show us some good?
Lift up the light of your face upon us, O LORD!"
PSALM 4:6 ESV

From ancient times people have been expecting someone, be it a god or a king, to lead them to good times. God wanted to be this leader for Israel, but they asked for judges and then they asked for a king.

These days we look to our government and point fingers at them for the way that our nation is headed. We still seem to ask the question "Who is going to lead us to any good?" God was hopeful that his people wouldn't look to earthy leaders for their guidance and wellbeing. Instead, he wanted to show his face to his people and have them trust that he would lead them into goodness. Can you trust him today?

Heavenly King, I know that you are the only one who can truly show your people the right and good way. Shine upon me today.

Ask for Life

He asked you for life, and you gave it to him—
length of days forever and ever.
PSALM 21:4 CSB

You wouldn't necessarily think to ask God for life because you are already living it. The reality of the human condition, however, was that we needed to be rescued. The curse of sin on humanity meant that we would ultimately destroy ourselves. Death was the natural consequence. So, humanity—in fact God's whole creation—asks for life!

When Jesus was resurrected, he not only showed that we have life but that our new life in him is forever. Be blessed this morning, knowing that he has graced you with eternity.

Jesus, sometimes I get so wrapped up in this life and the concerns of this world that I forget to think to the life beyond. Thank you so much for the gift of eternity. I will carry that blessing in my heart today.

Praising Together

You are enthroned as the Holy One;
you are the one Israel praises.
PSALM 22:3 NIV

When was the last time you were a part of a church service? For some of us it is every week, for others it is more sporadic. This habitual attendance might seem a little too religious for you, and yet there is something about coming together and worshipping God as a group of people. It would be hard to deny in those times that God is being worshipped and that he is the one we are all praising.

Even if you aren't attending church regularly, remember that you are not alone in your praise for the one true God.

Holy One, I am encouraged by remembering that there are so many other believers that are praising you right now with me. Thank you for churches and groups of people that are gathered together to acknowledge that you are worthy.

Mountaintops

LORD, when you favored me,
you made my royal mountain stand firm;
but when you hid your face,
I was dismayed.
PSALM 30:7 NIV

As you start your day, are you feeling full of God's favor or do you feel like he is absent from you? You might interpret those mountaintop moments as being in God's favor, but don't discount the times when you are dismayed. There is sometimes a greater blessing from the valleys that you might not fully comprehend while you are walking through it.

It is in your times of despair when you begin to be more aware of your need and dependency on God. It might feel like he has hidden his face but be assured that he is as present to you now as he is in the mountaintops. Seek him out today.

Lord, thank you that life isn't the same. Often I don't look to you when I am feeling safe and secure, but I know that you are there. I choose to trust that you are here even in times of dismay.

What You Hate

I hate those who cling to worthless idols;
as for me, I trust in the LORD.
PSALM 31:6 NIV

Hate is a very strong word. You might have been raised to not say that you hate anything, yet here we see it… in Scripture! What a great book God has given us. The Psalms share the raw emotions and human experiences with no qualifiers! We try so hard to do the right thing and say the right thing, but we need to give ourselves the freedom to express how we feel about situations.

You don't need to say it to anyone else, but you can direct your thoughts and words to God. The expression might just open the doorway for you to experience forgiveness and grace.

This morning, Lord, I am grateful for the freedom that I have in you to be myself. Often my words are just how I am feeling at the time, but I know that you understand that. Thank you that I am safe to be me.

Transcendent

*From his throne he observes
all who live on the earth.*
PSALM 33:14 NLT

It's been said that God is transcendent. We believe in a God who is above our world, beyond time and physical limitation, yet he is also so very near and personal to us.

Think about this aspect of God's character—he is transcendent: he is able to observe everything going on earth. What assurance does that provide for you as you go into your day?

Thank you, heavenly Father, for knowing all the activities of your creation. I reflect now on your character as King and ruler of all.

Only One Judge

Oh, let the evil of the wicked come to an end,
and may you establish the righteous—
you who test the minds and hearts,
O righteous God!
PSALM 7:9 ESV

When you say that a person is bad or good, or even determine what they are doing is bad or good, you are making a judgment based on your understanding of right and wrong. Humans have been doing this since they ate from the tree of the knowledge of good and evil.

This wasn't God's design for us. God is the only one who knows what is truly righteous and truly evil. That's why we can put our trust in him to make the call. He is the only one who knows and tests the minds and hearts of all people.

Righteous God, I am thankful that my judgement of things is not the final call. I am sorry for the times when I have made judgments that are not mine to make. Help me to continue to trust in your righteousness.

Empty Boasts

The wicked boasts of the desires of his soul,
and the one greedy for gain
curses and renounces the LORD.
PSALM 10:3 ESV

Our culture is one that values intelligence and an educated mind; philosophers and the great thinkers are among the highly esteemed. It can be easy to get caught up (or left behind!) in debates of religion, politics, and philosophy. The problem with worldly wisdom is that it is self-generated; it exists in the context of a finite mind that cannot grasp the mysteries of God.

The next time you feel yourself unable to answer the intellectual bully, ask yourself what the source of their wisdom is. Trust in the wisdom of Jesus—it is eternal and life-giving.

God, I trust that you have given me wisdom in my life. Help me to remember to use your wisdom and not the wisdom of this world in every decision I make.

Revealed in Nature

In his hand are the depths of the earth,
and the mountain peaks belong to him.
PSALM 95:4 NIV

It doesn't take much to marvel at creation. Looking up into the night sky, sitting on a shoreline, hiking through a forest, or watching a bud begin to blossom, our encounters with nature are many. But we don't often take the time to truly notice how incredible creation is.

Take a look around at God's creation today and dwell on the quality of God that is represented. Allow yourself time to reflect on God's divinity and eternal power and thank him for sharing it with you in a very real way.

Lord, open my eyes to the beauty of your creation around me. Allow me to see your qualities in all your created things.

A Way Out

How long must I struggle with anguish in my soul,
with sorrow in my heart every day?
How long will my enemy have the upper hand?
PSALM 13:2 NLT

One of the hardest realities of life is that we can't escape suffering. There is no easy fix to a heart or mind that has been broken or wounded in some way. You may be able to relate to an experience where you have felt sorrow in your heart every day. This could be about you, or perhaps it is about someone you love and cherish.

During those times of struggle, you desperately want a way out. It's important to cry out to God in these times and to acknowledge that you are totally dependent on him for help. Keep hoping and praying—he is a God that can be trusted.

Father, I am struggling with understanding the anguish that I am feeling. Please release me from my sorrow and help me to be patient in the process.

Perspective

*The L*ord* looks down from heaven on all mankind*
to see if there are any who understand,
any who seek God.
Psalm 14:2 niv

In a televised sports match, the referee can make a call that can
be challenged and proved otherwise by using camera footage to
replay the action. Here the replay can zoom in, go back and forth,
and analyze in slow motion to ultimately see what the call should
be. What the crowd or referee might have seen as one thing might
not be the truth and it is all a matter of perspective.

If we were to look at humanity through our own lens, we might see
it as a sad and desperate scenario. Just remember that God has his
own view and he sees every single thing. Let him be the one who
determines those who understand and are truly seeking him.

Lord, thank you that you have a much better perspective about
this world and the people in it than I do. Help me to be the kind of
person that seeks to understand you.

Freedom to Enter

Who may worship in your sanctuary, Lord?
Who may enter your presence on your holy hill?
PSALM 15:1 NLT

In ancient Israel, the sanctuary wasn't an easy place to enter. It was a place where the living God dwelled and there were requirements of sacrifice and purification before anyone could enter and be cleansed from sin. In that day, it was a selective process: a question worth considering by King David: "Who can worship in this sanctuary?"

We are so privileged that Jesus now lives within us, which makes us holy enough to be in the presence of God at any time. There's nothing you need to do but let Jesus in. Enjoy the freedom of being in the presence of God today.

Jesus, I feel so blessed to have such gracious access to your presence. I rely completely on your grace today and ask for a tangible sense of your presence with me throughout it.

Master and Mediator

*O my soul, you have said to the L*ORD,
*"You are my L*ORD,
My goodness is nothing apart from You."
PSALM 16:2 NKJV

We can be very smug about our accomplishments. You might have a good marriage, or comparatively well-behaved children. Perhaps you have been promoted at work or have been getting really good grades with your study. Even better, you might be using your gifts at church and tithing regularly. Good for you!

These things are wonderful and should be pursued, but don't lose sight of who all of this goodness really belongs to. You are good because you are following a good teacher, friend, and gracious shepherd of your soul. He doesn't accept you because you are good; you are good because you have been accepted.

Lord, you are my Lord. My goodness is nothing apart from you. Shepherd me throughout this day so I can share this goodness with the world.

Whispers at Night

I will bless the LORD who has advised me;
Indeed, my mind instructs me in the night.
PSALM 16:7 NASB

Have you ever woken up in the middle of the night with some clear thoughts or ideas about something? Our Creator has given us so many ways to be inspired and thoughtful about our lives. Sometimes our dreams help to give us clarity, or sometimes it is the simple still and quiet window in the night that gives us a good path forward.

If you have had these times, try to write down your thoughts or record them on your phone so you can reflect on it in the morning. Thank the Lord for counseling you and giving you an opportunity to hear him.

Holy Spirit, I don't always know when you are speaking to me and when I am just hearing my own thoughts. Give me discernment to know how you are working in my life.

Hiding

Finally, I confessed all my sins to you
and stopped trying to hide my guilt.
I said to myself, "I will confess my rebellion to the Lord."
And you forgave me! All my guilt is gone.
PSALM 32:5 NLT

The only time hiding might be fun is when you are playing a game of hide-and-seek. Any other form of hiding denotes that someone is worried about being found or being found out. It's interesting that we might hide our sin from God even when we know that freedom is only a confession away.

Consider the reasons you might hide your sin. Are you worried that you won't be forgiven? If that's the reason, read this verse again. God forgives you and takes away the guilt, every time! Another reason we hide sin is that we are worried about what other people might think of us. This is pride and will keep you feeling trapped. Stop trying to hide. Confess and release yourself from guilt—you are forgiven!

Jesus, I confess my sin to you right now. I'm sorry for hiding and not dealing with it. Help me to come clean so I can have freedom from guilt.

Anchored in Truth

The word of the LORD is right and true;
he is faithful in all he does.
PSALM 33:4 NIV

There are many moments of doubt in our Christian journey, and often those times arise when we are challenged about what we really believe. We ask questions about creation, our beginnings, and even how it works for Christ to have come into the world and save us.

It's ok to question and even to doubt, but don't lose hope and the expectation that Jesus is with you in the middle of your doubts. As this Scripture says, the Word of the Lord is right and true. Use this as a starting point for all your questions and let the Holy Spirit guide you to a place of confidence in your faith.

Lord, thank you that you are with me in my doubts. I choose to believe that your Word is right and true and that you will be faithful to help me through my questions.

Pursue Peace

Turn from evil and do good;
seek peace and pursue it.
PSALM 34:14 NIV

Living a peaceful existence is a struggle in our day and age. We have so much going on in our lives, competing with our time and energy. You might have a family to take care of, work piling up around you, study hanging over your head…maybe you have all of these at once!

On top of that we have social media and endless entertainment options to keep our minds busy. It's no wonder that we suffer from feeling stressed out and anxious. This can often result in us being argumentative and frustrated. If this sounds like you lately, remind yourself that peace is something that you need to pursue. It doesn't always come naturally, so ask the Holy Spirit for help.

Holy Spirit, I need your presence with me today so I can carry peace into my mind, body, and soul.

Bones

With every bone in my body I will praise him:
"LORD, who can compare with you?
Who else rescues the helpless from the strong?
Who else protects the helpless and poor
from those who rob them?"

PSALM 35:10 NLT

In times where we are grieved by injustice, we need to go to the one and only just King. It can be confusing to know when and how God intervenes and protects because we still experience darkness in our world and there are many who are helpless and poor.

God is working in our world and if you pay attention, you will notice the ways that he is using others to look out for those in need. He is a good God and there is no one like him, so praise him with every bone in your body!

Father, you created me with a lot of bones, so if every bone were to praise you it would last a long time! Encourage my heart and let me be a part of your plan to help the helpless.

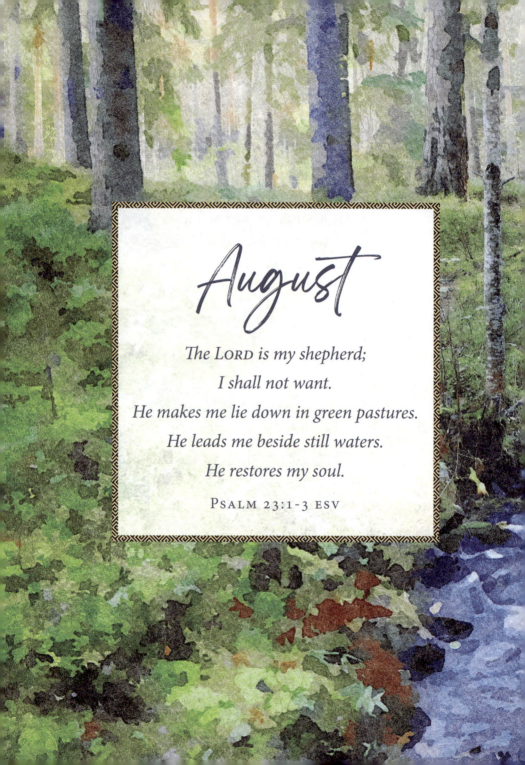

August

The LORD is my shepherd;
I shall not want.
He makes me lie down in green pastures.
He leads me beside still waters.
He restores my soul.

PSALM 23:1-3 ESV

Thirsty Soul

O God, you are my God;
earnestly I seek you;
my soul thirsts for you;
my flesh faints for you,
as in a dry and weary land
where there is no water.

PSALM 63:1 ESV

Our physical nature is not separate from our spiritual life. Sometimes when we are in such great need physically it's like our whole being is hungry, thirsty, or in pain. This is how David felt when he was in the wilderness—desperate for real food and water, yet feeling like his soul needed the same nourishment.

Waking up this morning, what did you feel like you needed? You probably aren't in the actual wilderness, but perhaps you needed a shower, coffee, or some breakfast. Let your needs today compel you to feel that same need for Christ.

Lord, I want to crave for you in the same way my body craves what it needs. I acknowledge that I desperately need you today.

Wishing Well

May he grant you your heart's desire
and fulfill all your plans.
PSALM 20:4 ESV

This verse sounds like some good words for a well-wishing greeting card! It's great to reflect on the positive words of others because more often than not, we genuinely do wish the best for other people and we do hope that their heart's desires and plans will be fulfilled.

Think of this verse as a prayer for you. May he grant you your heart's desire and fulfill all your plans.

Jesus, I am so glad that I have friends and family who really do hope and pray good things for my life. Thank you for giving me the encouragement that I need to start my day.

Unexpected Angels

The LORD hears good people when they cry out to him,
and he saves them from all their troubles.
PSALM 34:17 NCV

Sometimes your rescue can come in the form of another person. We cry out to God and ask him for help, but we shouldn't presume to know exactly how he is going to help us. God has humanity in his image and can express himself through people with their kind acts, words of encouragement, and often a great piece of advice or wisdom.

Thank God today for the people that he has put in your life and the unexpected ways that he can use them to encourage you.

Lord, I thank you so much for revealing yourself to me through others. Thank you that we can be a part of the healing and grace that you long to share with this broken world.

Good Habits

Oh, that my actions would consistently reflect your decrees!
PSALM 119:5 NLT

Wake up. Make bed. Get dressed. Coffee. Not always in that order, but you can guarantee that many do those things every single morning. They might also bite their nails, anger easily, or stay up too late. Patterns are hard to break. We are, after all, creatures of habit, and unfortunately not all habits are good.

What do you do when you are confronted with a habit that is not positive? Do you recognize when you rely on something just because it makes you feel accepted, comforted, or in control? Sometimes we aren't even conscious of our habits until we try to give them up. What habits do you know are unhealthy for your life?

Lord, I have some habits that I know are not the best for me. Give me wisdom today to discern those things that you want me to get rid of.

My Contribution

How good and pleasant it is
when God's people live together in unity!
PSALM 133:1 NIV

A tooth is such a small part of the body, but when it begins to ache, it can be debilitating! The human body is fascinating in this way. God has created all of our parts to be distinct yet interdependent.

As a Christ follower, you are part of the body of Christ. More important than trying to distinguish which part you are is the recognition of just how important your unique gifts are to the health of the whole body. You were created to belong to something that is greater than yourself.

Jesus, help me to understand my contribution to my family, my church, and my community. Let me recognize my unique gifts and use them for your glory.

The Good Lane

I am certain that I will see the LORD's goodness
in the land of the living.
PSALM 27:13 CSB

Do you ever catch yourself dwelling on the negative aspects of life? We can be nonchalant when someone tells us good news, but talk for hours about conflict, worries, and disappointment.

It is good to communicate things that aren't going so well in our lives, but we can also fall into the trap of setting our minds on the wrong things. Give your mind over to truth, honor, pure and lovely things today. You are sure to find goodness in unexpected places!

God, thank you for creating me with your goodness in my heart. If I am tempted today with negative talk or harmful gossip, I pray you would give me the wisdom and grace to resist the bad and choose good.

Fountain of Life

You are the fountain of life,
the light by which we see.
PSALM 36:9 NLT

People seem to always be trying to source their life in material things. We think if we can buy the right clothes or the latest phone, or hang out with influential people, we will find some satisfaction in life.

You might look forward to a vacation overseas or going out to eat at an expensive restaurant. All of these are there for your enjoyment, but they don't bring you the true source of life that you really need. Look to the light as your source of life and when you find him, let him light up the path ahead of you.

Jesus, help me to stop chasing material things that will soon fade. I choose to follow your everlasting fountain of life.

The Small Things

Your goodness is as high as the mountains.
Your justice is as deep as the great ocean.
LORD, you protect both people and animals.
PSALM 36:6 NCV

Are you an animal lover? You might have pets at home, or you might prefer to admire animals from a distance. If you own an animal, chances are you have probably prayed for that pet at some point and maybe felt a little unsure if God cared to answer you.

This verse is a great reminder that God created the entire universe, which goes beyond the mountains and oceans right to the smallest of creatures. It is all part of his creation. He loves it and he wants it protected.

Lord, thank you for the privilege of caring for the things you have created, be it a dog or a tree in the garden. Help me to protect and respect your creation.

Don't Envy Them

Don't worry about the wicked
or envy those who do wrong.
PSALM 37:1 NLT

Life is not fair and there are certainly many people who you could think of who are doing better than you in terms of their relative success. The Bible tries to teach us about the true meaning of success. It is not wealth, fame, or status that will bring you true joy.

It is easy to be envious of those who have these things though. When you see others seemingly getting ahead in life, you begin to fret about where you are at. Don't fall into the trap of comparing yourself with others; instead, thank God for the good things he has already provided you with.

Lord, help me to turn my complaints into thankfulness. Even if others seem to be doing better than I am, help me to see that my concerns are shallow and won't bring me life. Thank you for everything I have.

Innocence

He will bring forth your righteousness as the light,
and your justice as the noonday.
PSALM 37:6 ESV

Have you ever been accused of something you didn't do, or had rumors started about you that simply were not true? We are people who feel it is necessary to defend ourselves; we feel like we constantly need to explain our actions and behaviors to people or make excuses for the mistakes we make.

In the times you are feeling blamed and are gearing up to defend, remember that Jesus is the one who redeems you. What matters the most is your heart before him. Let him defend you; he is the one that has made you righteous and he will make that shine.

Jesus, help me to accept my mistakes and not worry too much when I am blamed for things I haven't done. Thank you that you come to my defense every time because you have made me blameless in your sight.

Bottled In

As I stood there in silence—
not even speaking of good things—
the turmoil within me grew worse.

PSALM 39:2 NLT

The psalmist here is describing one of those moments where you bottle up all of your emotions. Can you relate to those times where you are feeling so much turmoil on the inside, but you just can't find the words to express yourself?

You might over analyze how to say accurately what you feel, worried that it will come out in the wrong way. Maybe you get worried about how the people who hear you will react. The trouble is, turmoil grows when you can't let it out. If there isn't anyone around you who you can share with, direct your emotions toward Jesus. He will listen.

Thank you, Jesus, in times when I am bottling things up, I have a friend in you. I know you can handle anything I need to express.

Brief and Fleeting

Lord, remind me how brief my time on earth will be.
Remind me that my days are numbered—
how fleeting my life is.
PSALM 39:4 NLT

It can be a sobering reminder that our time on earth will come to an end, and as the years go on it's easier to feel as though our time here really is brief. But this isn't the end; it is only a part of the life that God has in store for you.

Don't get down about how fleeting this life is; it is here to be enjoyed and lived as fully as you can. Just remember that there is more joy that extends into eternity. Approach your day with the knowledge that when this life ends, a new, more joyous one begins.

Father, I need a fresh perspective for my day ahead. When I begin to get overly concerned about the small stuff, give me the capacity to stand back and know that life is too short to get so anxious.

Sacrificial Heart

You take no delight in sacrifices or offerings.
Now that you have made me listen, I finally understand—
you don't require burnt offerings or sin offerings.
PSALM 40:6 NLT

Our world rewards those who get things done. If you put in the effort and achieve results, you are commended for your success. Think of the marathon runner who puts in hours of training and works their body to the extreme. The idea of sacrifice in ancient times is similar. The harder it is to do, the more pleased others are with you. This is why it is always hard to accept that your salvation has got nothing to do with trying so hard!

God delights in your heart. He loves you for who you are. He doesn't require anything of you but a heart that seeks him.

Holy Spirit, thank you for being present with me this morning. I am in awe of the grace that I experience, and I will rest in the understanding that I don't have to do anything to please you. I just get to love you!

So Many Sins

Troubles without number surround me;
my sins have overtaken me, and I cannot see.
They are more than the hairs of my head,
and my heart fails within me.

PSALM 40:12 NIV

We've all done some pretty foolish things in our lifetime. You might be thinking of a time when you judged someone unnecessarily, or assumed one thing was happening when it actually wasn't. You may have made youthful promises that you certainly haven't kept!

Sometimes we have good intentions, other times we do not, but Scripture says when we realize our foolishness, it's time to admit our guilt.

Lord, I'm sorry for the foolish things that I have said and done. I know that you are gracious and kind, so I come to you with an honest heart, admitting my mistakes, knowing I am forgiven. Let me be a shining example of your love today.

Peaceful Sleep

I lie down and sleep;
I wake again, because the LORD sustains me.
PSALM 3:3-4 NIV

There is always something to worry about, isn't there? Whether it's health, finances, relationships, or details, there are many unknowns in life that can easily keep us worrying. What if we could trust completely that God would take care of us and our loved ones. God is our rock and he alone will sustain us.

There will be many unknowns in your life. There will be moments when the rug feels as though it's been pulled out from under you and there is nothing to do but despair. In those moments that you can't control, you can trust. You can rest your soul, your mind, and your body in the hands of the one who has the power to sustain you.

Lord, today I face the unknown. Let me rest in the knowledge that you will sustain me.

Feeling Trapped

The cords of the grave coiled around me;
the snares of death confronted me.
PSALM 18:5 NIV

This is our faith walk. While Jesus' light never goes out, sometimes our sight does. We get so bogged down by circumstances, by sin, by our own agendas, we can't see a thing.

So how do we keep moving? We cry out, and then we follow the sound of God's voice. We must step more slowly now, but we can still walk. We just need to listen and have faith in his voice.

Lord, I know that you are always ready to rescue me, but I also know that I need to acknowledge my distress, so I call out to you and plead with you to rescue me. Thank you for hearing my cry.

Lost Friends

My best and truest friend,
who ate at my table,
has even turned against me.
PSALM 41:9 NCV

It's got to be one of the most hurtful experiences to have a friend turn against you, but it does happen. There are many reasons why, and often they are linked with extreme circumstances that put friends under strain. Sometimes friendships become competitive and jealousy disrupts the equilibrium.

Whatever the reason, it can be life altering to lose your best and truest friend. If you have experienced this, take heart in the understanding that this world isn't perfect; people are not perfect, but God can and will redeem it all.

Jesus, today I need to be reminded of your desire to heal relationships and broken hearts. Thank you for my friends, even those who have hurt me deeply. I choose to forgive and allow healing to begin.

Troubled Times

The LORD also will be a refuge for the oppressed,
a refuge in times of trouble.
PSALM 9:9 NKJV

It feels easier to trust God in the big moments, the desperate moments. But what about the everyday moments—the times that we grab hold of control and want to do it all ourselves?

In those moments, we can press into him without restraint. Let go, cry out to him, ask him to carry you. And he will. The everyday moments that might feel crooked will be straightened. He will carry you as he promises.

Jesus, thank you for being my Good Shepherd. Help me to seek out your ways today in all the everyday decisions. I know you don't need to tell me what exactly to do but help me to be like you so I reflect your nature to others around me.

Call Waiting

I call to you, God, and you answer me.
Listen to me now, and hear what I say.
PSALM 17:6 NCV

If only answers to prayer came so simply or quickly. Perhaps you want to know what courses to study, what job offer to accept, what school your kids should go to.

God's Word encourages us again and again to come to him with our questions, concerns, and deepest longings. He does promise a reply, though not necessarily in the form of a check in a box.

God, I call to you now, asking for answers. At times I am unsure if I am asking the right thing, but I know it doesn't matter because you will hear me and you will answer, even if it isn't the answer that I want.

Floodwaters

*The L*ORD *rules over the floodwaters.*
*The L*ORD *reigns as king forever.*
PSALM 29:10 NLT

Picture a season in your life where you were knee-deep in busyness, swallowed in sadness, or buried in exhaustion. Picture that season and how you looked, acted, reacted, and survived.

Now picture the King of the heavens and earth. See how he rules over the entire earth. This powerful God wants you to lean on him, and that seems easy to do when you understand just how great and mighty he is. If you have woken up feeling tired, lean on the strength of your Savior.

Lord, I know what it is like to be weary and weak. Thank you that you have always been my strength and that you will be my source of power today.

Perpetual Praise

I will extol the LORD at all times;
his praise will always be on my lips.
PSALM 34:1 NIV

It's relatively easy to sing God's praises when all is going well in our lives: when he blesses us with something we asked for, when he heals us, or when he directly answers a prayer. We naturally turn and give him praise and glory for good things. What about when things aren't going well? What about in dry times, painful times, or times of waiting?

Choose today to have praise readily on your lips instead of complaint. Whenever you feel discontentment or frustration, replace it with praise. By focusing on the goodness of God, the hardships will lessen and your joy will increase.

Lord, I choose praise. My day has barely started and I can already feel the stresses mounting, but I choose praise. Let my lips be full of joy instead of complaint.

Groans and Sighs

I am feeble and severely broken;
I groan because of the turmoil of my heart.
PSALM 38:8 NKJV

Have you ever been run so ragged that you just didn't know if you could take even one more step? Your calendar is a blur of scheduled activities, your days are full, your every hour is blocked off for this or that, and it's hard to find a spare minute for yourself. Even your bones feel weary, and you fall into your bed at night, drained from it all.

Are you allowing the Lord to guide your days? Though you may be weary or heartbroken, he has enough energy to get you through it all. Hold out your hand to him today and walk side-by-side with Jesus.

Father, you know exactly where my heart is and how I am feeling right now. You understand me more than anyone in this life because you created me. Help me to know that I am understood.

Quietly Waiting

For God alone, O my soul,
wait in silence,
for my hope is from him.
PSALM 62:5 ESV

If the radio were broken in your car, would you need to fix it immediately, or would you relish the silence? Perhaps you or someone you know keeps the TV on all day "for the noise."

What is it about silence that makes so many of us uncomfortable? Some of us even talk to ourselves to avoid it. Seek out silence today. Allow God to discern your needs and your questions, and then wait for him to answer.

God, allow me some time of silence. Right now I wait on you. Even if you don't speak, let me feel your presence so I can be restored in silence.

Hear and Protect

Bend down, O Lord, and hear my prayer;
answer me, for I need your help.
PSALM 86:1 NLT

In this world full of independence, we have not had to practice the art of asking for help. None of us want to impose ourselves on anyone; we don't want to make a fuss, and we think we should be able to do things on our own.

But God didn't create you to be on your own, or have to do things by yourself. Today, ask him for answers, ask him for help, ask him for protection and trust that he will save you.

Bend down, O Lord, and hear my prayer; answer me when I need your help. Protect me when I feel afraid; save me when I feel I am falling. I serve and trust you today because you are my God.

You Are Near

You are near, O LORD,
and all your commands are true.
PSALM 119:151 NLT

The sun will set tonight; it will rise tomorrow. This is truth. We have no reason to doubt what we've witnessed every day of our lives. But when experience tells us otherwise, or perhaps we have no experience to go on, doubts creep in.

It's going to snow tomorrow. "I doubt that," we say. Remember today that God's truth is unchanging. It is sure as the sun that rose this morning.

God, just as the psalmist wrote, you are near me always, so close to me. Thank you that every one of your commands reveals truth. Let me trust in your truth as I go into my day.

Compassion for All

The LORD is good to all;
he has compassion on all he has made.
PSALM 145:9 NIV

Have you ever laid in bed at night thinking over past wrongdoings and beating yourself up over decisions you made years ago? If so, you are not alone. We can be incredibly hard on ourselves.

There is good news for us all. Once we accept Christ as our Savior, we are made new. There is no need to continue to berate ourselves for the choices of the past. He has washed away our sins and made us clean. We don't have to look at life from our former point of view because our old lives are gone, and new ones have begun.

Thank you, Almighty God, for your forgiveness. You forget the past, so help me to move forward in this new day and this new life you have given me.

Good Stories

My mouth will tell of your righteous deeds,
of your saving acts all day long—
though I know not how to relate them all.
PSALM 71:15 NIV

There are many people in this world who can tell a good story. It is a gift to captivate an audience, or persuasively present your point of view. It's precisely because it is a gift that not all of us are created equal in our use and skill with words.

You may be part of the majority of people who find it difficult to communicate exactly what you want to say, but that doesn't stop the majority of us from communicating! When you are excited or thankful or have good news, you will tell it any way that you can. The next time you are blessed by God's goodness or grace, make a point of sharing it, even if the words don't flow as well as you would like.

Jesus, you have been so good and kind to me. Give me the boldness to express how good you are to others in my life today.

Restored

Though you have made me see troubles, many and bitter,
you will restore my life again;
from the depths of the earth you will again bring me up.
PSALM 70:20 NIV

It may be a relief to know that other people have experienced troubles and know that God has allowed it to happen. We may have grown up with an expectation that God will keep us safe from all troubles, and then we find it hard to reconcile when we face hardships.

You might be experiencing some of those troubles right now—in your family, at work, or in your social circles. Be encouraged that even though those times feel bitter, God is still at work in you and longing for restoration in your life and in the lives of others. Trust that he will bring you out of your circumstance and you will be restored once again.

God, thank you for being with be during my many troubles. Bring peace to my heart today as I confidently trust in your restoration.

Even the Birds

Even the sparrow finds a home,
and the swallow a nest for herself,
where she may lay her young,
at your altars, O LORD of hosts, my King and my God.
PSALM 84:3 ESV

The expanse of God's kingdom is never ending; it is a kingdom that is open and safe for all to enter, even the smallest of the creatures. God's kingdom is inclusive and doesn't concern itself with who is in and who is out. This is a great model for the way that we should live.

People need to feel included about every aspect of who they are: age, race, and yes, even political party! As a representative of the kingdom of Christ, we need to ensure people are getting a consistent message that all are welcome.

Jesus, thank you for the example that you set while you were on earth; an example that showed us all that you will happily sit with anyone and make them feel welcome. Help me to be an includer today.

Students

Teach me your way, Lord,
that I may rely on your faithfulness;
give me an undivided heart,
that I may fear your name.
PSALM 86:11 NIV

What were you like as a student at school? Some students are focused on the tasks and can listen well, especially if it's a subject they are interested in. Others find themselves getting distracted by the more social aspects of school, or they aren't interested in what they are being taught, or perhaps they just genuinely don't understand.

When it comes to Christ, it's important to let yourself be taught. To follow in his way shouldn't be boring; it is life-giving and well worth paying attention to. Give him your undivided heart today.

Jesus, as I go through my day, help me to be a student that pays attention to what you are teaching me. Let me be observant and responsive to your guidance.

Show Me a Sign

Show me a sign of your favor,
that those who hate me may see
and be put to shame because you, Lord,
have helped me and comforted me.
PSALM 86:17 ESV

Do you find it hard to know when God is actually speaking to you and when it might just be your own thoughts? When we are seeking answers for a way out of a situation or in a place of real uncertainty, we often want to know exactly what to do. Our choices have consequences and we can be paralyzed because we don't want to make the wrong choice. This is when we bargain with God and ask him for a sign! We can throw all kinds of things at him in our desperation to know what to do.

Be encouraged that God will help, and he is in the middle of all of your decision-making processes. He might not give you an exact sign, but he will be leading your heart and your thoughts in the right direction. Trust that he is in the process.

God, I need your guidance in difficult moments of indecision. Help me to trust that you will lead me on the right path.

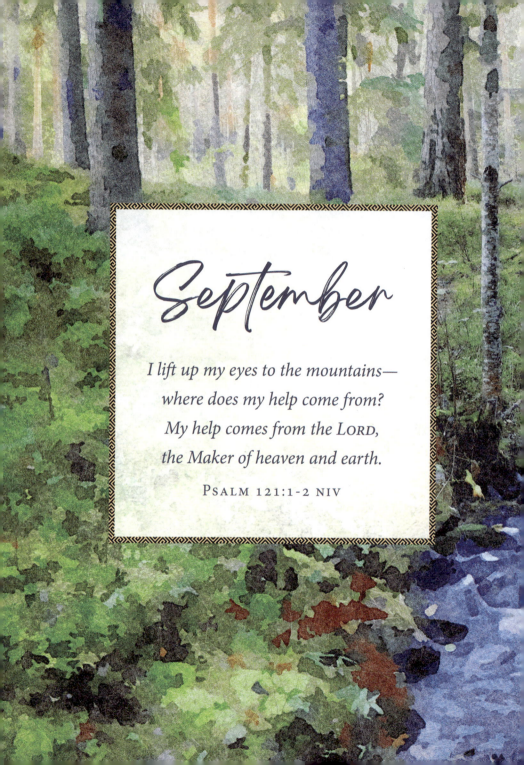

September

*I lift up my eyes to the mountains—
where does my help come from?
My help comes from the LORD,
the Maker of heaven and earth.*

PSALM 121:1-2 NIV

Unburdened

I removed the burden from their shoulders;
their hands were set free from the basket.
PSALM 81:6 NIV

Life can seem like one job after the next. Responsibility is our burden, weighing us down with work, childcare, bills, home maintenance, and everything in between. Before you start complaining, it's good to be reminded that we have choices and have not been forced into these jobs in the way the Israelites were when they were in slavery for hundreds of years!

When God released his people from their forced labor, the freedom they experienced would have been surreal. Be thankful today for your freedom despite the tasks that will keep you busy throughout your day.

Lord, I am grateful that you do not long for anyone to be in slavery and that you set your people free so long ago. Help me to enjoy my responsibilities today and to wear them lightly as I remember my freedom.

Pilgrimage

Blessed are those whose strength is in you,
whose hearts are set on pilgrimage.
PSALM 84:5 NIV

We never really arrive at our spiritual destination of holiness and that's the way it is meant to be. The beauty is found where the heart is inclined toward finding the presence of God. This is our journey of faith in Christ. It is a pilgrimage in every sense of the word.

It might be a long and difficult terrain to navigate, but there will be wonders to see along the way and some profound insights and thoughts as you progress. This pilgrimage is one that ends at the most beautiful of places, one that your heart cannot fully comprehend. Enjoy the journey that you are on today.

Jesus, thank you my eternal destination is full of promise. I also want to thank you for this journey that is leading me there. Help me to appreciate the beauty of the walk today.

Congregation

Praise the LORD!
I will give thanks to the LORD with my whole heart,
in the company of the upright, in the congregation.
PSALM 111:1 ESV

God had a purpose to fulfil through the people of Israel. He intended this community of people to be part of revealing his plan for humanity. They needed to reconnect with one another so they could be unified in their covenant with the one true God.

There is a certain specialness to reuniting with our family and friends on those occasions we can all be together in one place. When we are together with people who share the same values, stories, and even similar humor, it makes life feel more meaningful. Think about the community that you feel closest to, and make an effort to get in touch today.

Thank you, Lord, that you don't want us to do life alone. Thank you that there is strength and unity in the gathering of people who love one another. Give me a chance today to connect with others so we can enjoy and encourage each other.

Honor His Name

Help us, O God of our salvation!
Help us for the glory of your name.
Save us and forgive our sins
for the honor of your name.
PSALM 79:9 NLT

God cares about how he reveals himself to the world. His name was made great because of the favor he showed Israel in releasing them from slavery in Egypt. There were many times God could have allowed the people of Israel to destroy themselves, but instead he protected them, and in doing so, he showed the nations his nature of mercy.

You are God's chosen representative of earth, and today you have the opportunity to reveal some of his merciful nature to others. It is not something to feel pressured about; rather, it is a privilege that you carry to be able to honor his name.

God, you are a God of mercy, and I have witnessed that in your Scriptures and also in my life. Let me reveal this nature to others as I act in kindness and goodwill toward people today.

The Temple Within

O God, the nations have come into your inheritance;
they have defiled your holy temple;
they have laid Jerusalem in ruins.
PSALM 79:1 ESV

The Israelites expected that once God had shown up in the temple he would never leave. It would have been devastating then, when the temple was ultimately destroyed. The problem with their expectation was that they had placed their hope in a physical building.

How wonderful that God kept his promise of dwelling forever with his people by allowing Jesus to put that temple into our hearts. You are now a beautiful dwelling for God's presence, and he is willing to fill you with his glory. Receive his presence and let it influence all that you do today.

Holy Spirit, I receive your presence right now. Thank you for the refreshing sense of peace that will help me to have a blessed day. Let people recognize that my peace comes from you.

Just and Good

All he does is just and good,
and all his commandments are trustworthy.
PSALM 111:7 NLT

We might have a picture of God that is two-sided. We can think of him as a God who is good but also a God of justice. We like to separate these two truths about God as if they are opposite sides— one full of graciousness and the other full of making sure the rules are kept.

That's not what this verse says, though, it says that all he does is just and good. This means that everything God does on earth and in your life is an outworking of grace and righteousness. Think of it another way: rules are not there just so that we can define a mistake; they are there to keep everyone safe and well. This is justice and goodness hand-in-hand, and you can trust his ways.

Lord, thank you for reminding me that you everything you do is both just and good. Help me to live by your commandments today, knowing that this is your grace at work in my life.

His Awesome Name

He provided redemption for his people;
he ordained his covenant forever—
holy and awesome is his name.

PSALM 111:9 NIV

As you wake to another morning, do you feel free from burdens or worn down by them? You might be experiencing some mountaintop moments and mornings are a joy, but if you are in a valley, mornings can be difficult.

Whatever your experience is right now, remember that God has redeemed you. He didn't just set the Israelites free, he set all of humanity free and made his promise of grace last forever. Let this covenant remind you of how awesome he is today so you are able to experience the light of this new life.

Jesus, thank you so much for your redemption that has not only set me free, but has set the world free. Help me be a part of sharing this good news to those in my life.

Wisdom in Doing

The fear of the LORD is the beginning of wisdom;
all those who practice it have a good understanding.
His praise endures forever!
PSALM 111:10 ESV

Wisdom is something everyone wants to have, yet many lack the ability to go beyond just knowing. This verse makes it pretty clear: wisdom is not just knowing about God's words; it is putting them into practice.

Sometimes we don't understand why God is guiding us in a certain direction or we don't quite understand the Scriptures. But if we start to put the words of God into practice, we will begin to understand more and more. This is how we grow in wisdom. We simply do it, and if we happen to make a mistake, we try again. True wisdom is in the doing.

Lord, I am blessed to have a little bit of knowledge about your ways. Help my understanding to grow as I put it into practice.

Parades

Enter his gates with thanksgiving,
and his courts with praise!
Give thanks to him;
bless his name!
PSALM 100:4 ESV

Have you ever been a part of a street or city parade to celebrate a sports team or local hero? You might have watched them on television, or been to a park with people singing, dancing, and cheering. This is the kind of picture we have of the people of God coming into God's kingdom and celebrating him as King!

You probably won't celebrate God with this kind of fanfare today, but remember him as King and celebrate him in the best way you know how.

Holy King, I choose to celebrate you today by having a heart that is joyful about your presence. I want to bless you with my words and actions.

Appearance

I will be careful to live a blameless life—
when will you come to help me?
I will lead a life of integrity in my own home.
PSALM 101:2 NLT

How has your home life been this morning? You might be in a phase of life where you are rushing around trying to get yourself ready for the day; perhaps you have kids that you are trying to feed, clothe, and get out the door for school. Life can be chaotic from the get-go, and it's hard to have integrity when you are feeling rushed and stressed.

Lean on the Lord for help so you have a bit more self-control than usual. If you are having a relaxed morning, use your peace to benefit the rest of your home. You will never achieve perfection, but it is worth pursuing for the sake of the people you live with.

Jesus, I am thankful that I have people around me to practice my integrity and self-control. Thank you for your grace. Please help me to have grace for others too.

Healer

He heals the brokenhearted
and bandages their wounds.
PSALM 147:3 NLT

Whether you are carrying pain and suffering from past abuse or tragedy, or you've more recently been hurt, run toward the one who heals. There is no requirement or need too great; he will piece you back together.

Your offering of praise to him is beautiful, and he will turn your mourning into joy.

Lord, I come to you as a person who has been broken and hurt by others. Sometimes I feel this pain more acutely than other times, but wherever I am with this, you know the things that have really torn my heart. Give me peace today, knowing that you are helping me to forgive and become whole again.

A Good Neighbor

Whoever slanders his neighbor secretly
I will destroy.
Whoever has a haughty look and an arrogant heart
I will not endure.
PSALM 101:5 ESV

We all love a good piece of gossip. Some might think that they are not prone to gossip, yet we all eagerly listen to it.

The next time you find yourself engaging in a conversation that involves whispers and low voices about someone else, ask yourself how the other person would feel if they knew others were talking about them. This is a quick strategy that will avoid you making the wrong choice to engage in further negative talk. Instead of engaging, put an end to it!

Lord, I am sorry when I have eagerly soaked up negative talk about others. Help me to bravely confront gossip and to always defend those who cannot defend themselves.

Inner Circle

My innermost circle will only be those
whom I know are pure and godly.
They will be the only ones I allow to minister to me.
Psalm 101:6 TPT

Humans were created for relationship; we are hardwired to want and need others. Because of our design, friendships are vitally important to us and also to our walk with God. Friends either bring us up or drag us down. Likewise, friends either encourage or discourage us in our pursuit of godliness.

As we seek counsel from our friends for the decisions we make in life, it is important that those friends are pushing us to follow Christ and not our own desires.

Jesus, I know that you desire that I have good friends. Give me discernment even today to spend time with the people who are good and uplifting and to keep away from the company of the unwise.

Lost Sight

LORD, hear my prayer!
Listen to my plea!
PSALM 102:1 NLT

Do you ever feel like you can't feel God? Like you've lost sight of him somehow? Sometimes we aren't sure how to get back to that place where we feel his presence strongly and hear his voice clearly.

God will not push himself on you. He will not share his glory with another, and he will not try to compete with the world for your heart. But if you draw near to him, he will wrap you in the power of his presence. Welcome him into your life today.

Lord, be close to me today. There have been times I don't know where you are or what you are doing, but I recognize that those are probably the times when I am not drawing close to you. Let me feel your presence surround me in all that I do.

Sunrise Brilliance

A light shines in the dark for honest people,
for those who are merciful and kind and good.
PSALM 112:4 NCV

Darkness can happen in various forms, be it a global crisis, workplace redundancies, a loss of home, or a personal collapse of a friendship. In these times, we desperately need the mercy and kindness of those around us. They can be the shining light that we need in our darkness.

In the same way, you can be that light to someone who is going through a moment of darkness. Pray about your own darkness, and then turn your prayers toward the difficult situations of those around you. Be an honest, merciful, kind, and good person, and watch Christ breakthrough in each circumstance.

Jesus, I am so grateful that your presence in my heart can help me to become a beacon of light in the midst of darkness. Help your mercy and kindness shine through me and intervene in the lives of those who are struggling so we can see hope emerge from the shadows.

Fair Business

*Good comes to those who lend money generously
and conduct their business fairly.*
PSALM 112:5 NLT

Money drives most of our decisions, challenges, and lifestyle. That's why we all need to be reminded to be careful with how much we value and trust in money. We don't have to neglect money, we just need to have a willingness to be generous so we don't become people who hold too tightly to what God has given us to steward appropriately.

You will no doubt spend money today. Make sure that you think about giving money, too. Be generous and fair, and money won't have a hold on you.

God, I know that I can become obsessed, stressed, and even selfish with money. Give me the wisdom and perspective to not hold too tightly to things that could ultimately steal my joy. Help me to find an opportunity to challenge my generosity today!

East to West

Everywhere—from east to west—
praise the name of the LORD.
PSALM 113:3 NLT

We live in a culturally diverse world, but often we are afraid to accept the way in which other cultures worship Christ. Our Scripture is full of the truth that Jesus came to free everyone from the curse and that his gift of eternal life was for every human, regardless of race, gender, or any other human distinctions.

Try to embrace the cultures around you because Jesus wants to be celebrated from all corners of the world—from one side right to the other. Praise him in your own way, but love the way others praise him too.

Jesus, help me to me more accepting of other cultures and the way they express their praise to you. Give me a heart that acknowledges that I am just one race of many and that we are all one in Christ.

Keep Out

Do not let my heart be drawn to what is evil
so that I take part in wicked deeds
along with those who are evildoers;
do not let me eat their delicacies.
PSALM 141:4 NIV

The world can offer a lot of great things. Careers offer success, relationships offer security, and riches can provide comfort. Nothing is inherently wrong with having these things, unless they are used for our own glory.

In the world, people want to glorify themselves. Thankfully, Jesus knew that the kingdoms of this world were nothing like the kingdom of God. He chose something greater. Are you able to resist the temptation of the world today?

Lord, thank you that you understand the temptations in this world. Please strengthen me for the day ahead and remind me that your kingdom is better than all the false glory that may come my way.

Burning the Candle

It is in vain that you rise up early and go late to rest,
eating the bread of anxious toil;
for he gives to his beloved sleep.
PSALM 127:2 ESV

There are days where you might wake up a little more sluggish, with a little less energy and positivity about the day. That can feel kind of empty, a gap you're hoping to fill.

The great thing about the God you serve is that in him you can be complete. He can be the gap filler. As you sit with him, his light begins to burn brighter.

Lord, lift me up this morning. It's hard to get out of bed and sometimes I feel anxious or worried about the day ahead. Give me energy and strength to face another day.

The Great Escape

The LORD brought his people out of Egypt,
loaded with silver and gold;
and not one among the tribes of Israel even stumbled.
PSALM 105:37 NLT

The story of Israel's rescue from hundreds of years of slavery in Egypt is not to be thought of lightly. What a miracle that God's chosen people were finally delivered.

There were generations after generations that were born and died in slavery, and finally this was the generation that God set free. Not only were they set free, but he loaded them with silver and gold and made it easy for them to escape. What a powerful God we serve!

Father God, sometimes these stories seem so far away in history that I don't relate to them. Today I am reminded that you are a God of yesterday, today, and forever. Be as present to me this day as you were to your people hundreds of years ago.

Shared Heritage

Let me share in the prosperity of your chosen ones.
Let me rejoice in the joy of your people;
let me praise you with those who are your heritage.
PSALM 106:5 NLT

There was a time when God had a chosen people, a special community that he would use to bear witness to his love and mercy. This group of people failed time after time, and we might wonder why God persisted with them.

Could it be that this is exactly why God used that nation? Through Israel, God showed us that his love extends far beyond our mistakes. The promise for this people is now a promise of prosperity and eternal life for all people. You don't have to ask to be a part of this kingdom; you already are, so rejoice!

Lord, thank you that I have become a chosen one! I am so glad to be accepted as part of this beautiful family that will share in your eternal kingdom.

Time to Eat

*They soon forgot what he had done
and did not wait for his plan to unfold.*
PSALM 106:13 NIV

When you are asked about what you had for breakfast, can you even remember? With minds that are often full of so many things, forgetfulness can threaten to derail your appointments, friendships, and even your relationship with Jesus. It's not that Jesus will ever depart from you, but if you quickly forget the good and gracious things he has done, you are less likely to spend time communicating with him.

It is often in our moments of greatest joy that we forget about the source of that joy. Give yourself some space today to remember Jesus and what he has done in your life.

Jesus, I am so grateful for all the times you have provided me with wisdom, peace, and assurance. I am grateful for the provision of a roof over my head and people around me that care for me. Help me to remember your goodness today and every day.

Love Wins

In return for my love they accuse me,
but I give myself to prayer.
PSALM 109:4 ESV

The ways of this world are different from the ways of the kingdom of God. Jesus made this clear by contrasting what the world says to do with your enemies and what Christ-followers should do. You probably have people in your mind that you see as a threat, or those who are unkind toward you. Sometimes we even get mocked for our faith, whether overtly or subtly. These are the very people that Christ asks us to love.

It's not easy to pray for those who have hurt you. Jesus understands this; he had to forgive all who brought him to his painful death on the cross. Allow Christ to be your strength as you practice goodness to those who have wronged you.

Lord, I need your help with loving my enemies. Give me your heart for them. Help me to see that everyone is loved by you no matter what they do or say. I don't accept their wrong behavior, but I choose today to pray for their healing, forgiveness, and restoration.

Secret Places

The secret of the Lord is for those who fear Him,
And He will make them know His covenant.
PSALM 25:14 NASB

Cherish the secret things. So much of our life is for others. Whether it is the requirement of jobs, keeping up relationships, or the programs we volunteer for, so much of our time and energy is spent on other people.

God wants your time. He wants it for you and for him. Maybe this will require a designated prayer closet or a quiet place away. Cherish alone time with him today.

Lord, I pray that I don't become religious with the way I spend time with you. I want to engage with you at any moment of any day, and I don't need it to be loud and pretentious. Let me be genuine in my prayers to you.

Your Perfect Words

*I've learned that there is nothing perfect
in this imperfect world except your words,
for they bring such fantastic freedom into my life!*
PSALM 119:96 TPT

Each of us is keenly aware of our own weaknesses. We know all our flaws too well and we make eliminating them our goal. But no matter how much effort we put in, we can never and will never achieve perfection. Despite most of us realizing that we will never be perfect, we still put unreasonable pressure on ourselves.

Whether in a task, in character, or in our walk with Christ, we easily become frustrated when we reach for perfection and can't grasp it. But if we allow perfectionism to drive our performance then we will quench our own potential and inhibit our effectiveness.

Lord, thank you that this life is not about my perfection but about yours. I will do my best to imitate your glory and excellence, but I know that this only comes by your grace. Help me to experience this today.

Enduring Kingdom

Blessed be the LORD God of Israel,
from everlasting to everlasting.
Amen and amen.
PSALM 41:13 CSB

Sometimes the Israelites won and sometimes they lost. This meant that their kings and kingdoms would often be abundant but they would also be annihilated. All along, Israel awaited a kingdom that would never fail or come to an end; a kingdom where God was eternally present.

In life, you will have experienced successes and failures, but be assured today that you are part of God's eternal kingdom that will stand forever.

God, I thank you that I can endure my failures knowing that ultimately I am part of a kingdom that will succeed. I put my hope in you and not the things of this world today.

Awake at Night

I lie awake,
I have become like a solitary bird on a housetop.
PSALM 102:7 NASB

Have you ever had one of those nights when you just didn't feel like you slept at all? Perhaps you kept checking the clock and seeing that only an hour had passed since the last time you checked. These nights can be laden with anxiety. No one else is awake and you are alone with your thoughts and feelings.

If you could picture that bird alone on a housetop, it would look a lot like you are feeling in those moments: solitary, waiting, watching. In those times of feeling alone, remember that your God is a God who never sleeps. He cares so much for you that he is ready to listen to your heart at any time. Use it as an opportunity to engage your Creator and get some insight and wisdom from him.

Father, thank you for caring for me even more than you care for the lonely bird on a rooftop. Help me to listen to you in those moments of loneliness.

Young Again

*He satisfies me with good things
and makes me young again, like the eagle.*
PSALM 103:5 NCV

It's interesting to compare youth to an eagle. Perhaps you would more think of your youth as a baby chick or a little duckling. An eagle is bold, daring, and soars freely across the skies. This is the picture that God wants to bring to your attention.

As you get prepared for another day, think of the good things that he has satisfied your life with. It might be your spouse, your children, your pet, or perhaps it's just that first cup of coffee that makes you feel like life is good! Cherish those things this morning so that you can be energized, bold and free.

Heavenly Father, thank you for satisfying me with so many good things. Restore my energy today so I can feel young and full of life.

Created Creatures

O LORD, how manifold are your works!
In wisdom you have made them all;
the earth is full of your creatures.
PSALM 102:24 NRSV

If you have ever watched a nature documentary, you will know what it is like to be fascinated by the creature that is being described. If you are capable of being captivated by one creature, imagine just how much there is to learn about every other creature out there!

This world is an incredible place, teeming with imagination and inspiration. Today is not just another ordinary day. Take some time to notice the extraordinary in what God has created in the living things around you.

O Lord, you have created such incredible things. Thank you for the inspiration that noticing your beauty can give me.

Waterfalls

He makes springs pour water into the ravines;
it flows between the mountains.
PSALM 104:10 NIV

The way that God takes care of his creation can be pretty astounding. Think of the way that he provides fresh water for the animals that live in those mountains. Your heavenly provider wants to bring you fresh water this morning. Maybe you have felt weighed down by work or home responsibilities or overwhelmed by your financial situation. You might just be feeling bored with very little joy or contentment in your heart.

Let God pour fresh water into the ravines of your soul this morning. Drink deeply from his love and mercy for you so you are revived for the coming day.

Holy Spirit, thank you for meeting me where I am this morning. Bring me your water of life so I can be refreshed and nourished today.

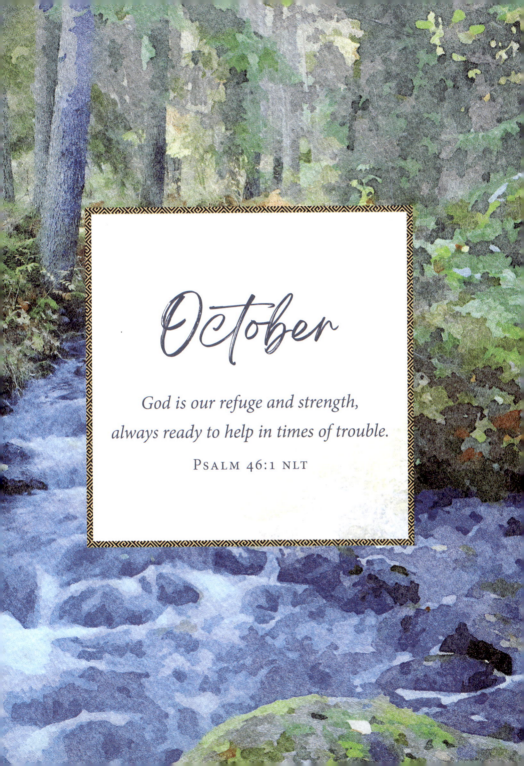

October

God is our refuge and strength,
always ready to help in times of trouble.

Psalm 46:1 nlt

Garbage Dump

He lifts the poor from the dust
and the needy from the garbage dump.
PSALM 113:7 NLT

Have you ever seen poverty so real that someone's home resembles a garbage dump? It can be heartbreaking to realize the kind of conditions that people live in, and often these situations are not too far from where we live.

God has a soft heart for those who are poor and needy, and as his image bearers the wellbeing of the poor should affect us too. If you are in a position to give to someone in need today, offer your time and money generously to further the cause of God's kingdom.

Jesus, today I might need your help to show generosity and goodwill toward people who are in desperate need of help. Give me the opportunity and wisdom to know how to help.

Not to Us

Not to us, LORD,
not to us but to your name be the glory,
because of your love and faithfulness.
PSALM 115:1 NIV

It's easy to accept the accolades of people when things that you have been involved in have gone well. We like our ideas and plans to succeed, and we like to be acknowledged for the good we have done. But things can start to become self-inflated when we give ourselves too much credit and become puffed up with pride.

It's always more important to remember where your success came from—the goodness and grace of God in your life. You can accept praise, but pass it on to the one who is truly worthy because we really can do nothing good without his love and faithfulness.

Thank you, Jesus, for the gifts you have given me to enable me to do good things on this earth. Let me be reminded to always give you the glory.

Your Desires

Delight yourself in the LORD,
and he will give you the desires of your heart.
PSALM 37:4 ESV

It is hard to reconcile some of the promises in God's Word with our disappointment with things that we have asked for but haven't yet received. Perhaps you are waiting for an answer or are hoping for a miracle.

Be encouraged that Jesus says that we need to be persistent and resilient and that he is always willing to open the door to you so you can find him. When you allow Jesus into your life, you will receive all that you need.

Jesus, I ask for a resilient mind so I can keep asking, knocking, and seeking in faith that I will find what I need. I put my trust in you, knowing that you care for me and that you open the door to answer me. Encourage my faith in you as I head into my day.

Idols

The unbelievers worship what they make—
their wealth and their work.
PSALM 115:4 TPT

You might be able to remember the time when you were not a Christian or not following the ways of Christ. In Bible times, people served other gods because they wanted health, wealth, and all forms of prosperity.

Instead of serving stone idols, we can be lured into finding other ways to achieve prosperity, from beauty products to the pursuit of high paying jobs. God's ways direct us in different forms of prosperity like healthy relationships, healing, and strength of character. Serve the Lord in sincerity and truth; his ways will give you all you need!

Lord, I am so often drawn to the things that make me feel better; yet I recognize that some of these things are shallow and not truly fulfilling. I come to you now in sincerity and truth, and I choose to serve you to the best of my ability.

History of Love

Those who are wise will take all this to heart;
they will see in our history the faithful love of the LORD.
PSALM 107:43 NLT

It can be heartbreaking to read the failure of Israel to remain faithful to God. It is like watching a movie where everything is going wrong and you want the characters to see that they are headed for disaster! Just when God sets them back on track, they choose to go back to their past mistakes.

We recognize this pattern in ourselves. There are times when we realize that we are making the same mistake again. God is calling you forward into his promises; don't go back!

God, you are so loving. I know that you saved your people because of this great love. I believe I am forgiven for my past mistakes and I ask that you help me to move forward into the good things you have called me to.

Delivered from Doom

He sent out his word and healed them,
and delivered them from their destruction.
PSALM 107:20 ESV

When you face trouble, hardship, or just need help, where do you turn to first? We have many things in this world that promise to bring us just what we need: diet plans, self-help books, and the varied advice received from friends, social media, and television.

Even though we know that God is faithful, he is not often the one we seek out first. When we are really in trouble, it is only God who can help.

Lord, today I choose to seek you first. Help me to notice those things that are distractions to the real help and guidance that I need from you. I don't want to be like the Israelites and frustrate you with serving other things. Keep me on your true path.

Instructions of Joy

I desire to do your will, my God;
your law is within my heart.
Psalm 40:8 niv

Once you have learned how to drive, you don't have to keep revisiting the learner's manual. The road rules become instinctive: you don't think too much about stopping at the stop sign or giving way to the person who is turning.

In the same way, the more we learn about following Christ, the more his ways become a part of our hearts. We make better decisions and treat others with respect because we know and enjoy doing Christ-like things. Take some time to learn about Jesus this morning so you bring more of him into your heart and your day.

Jesus, help me to know more about you so my actions and attitudes are in line with your Word.

Battle Lands

O Lord, my Lord, the strength of my salvation,
you have covered my head in the day of battle.
PSALM 140:7 ESV

Like all things in nature, our lives are always changing. Some seasons are much harder than others. There are times when we are experiencing battles, perhaps in our relationships, as parents, at work, with study, or maybe even an illness. We have to battle our emotions, fears, doubts, and anything else that seems to compete with our peace and happiness.

Turn to God, your strength and salvation, in these times of battle. He will cover your head so you are not devastated during this time. Hold on to hope that he will help get you through this.

Lord, when I am battling to get through these times, please protect my head and my heart. Sometimes my emotions seem overwhelming, and in these times, I ask that you rescue me from the wrong thoughts and direct my heart toward your truth and light.

Righteous Rebuke

Let the righteous strike me; it shall be a kindness.
And let him rebuke me;
It shall be as excellent oil;
Let my head not refuse it.
For still my prayer is against the deeds of the wicked.
PSALM 141:5 NKJV

When someone wise corrects you, it might be hard, but it should feel right. People who are full of God's wisdom lead you toward better pastures. They know what is ultimately better for you. The next time someone you trust rebukes you, instead of reacting out of hurt, take some time to think through what they have said, and ponder if it's something God would want to say to you right now.

Words from those who have selfish plans or evil intent will not feel right, and you can swiftly ignore those. Ask God to help you know the difference between righteous and wicked guidance.

Holy Spirit, give me discernment when others are giving me advice. Let me take hard words from righteous people with grace, knowing that they only want what is best for me.

Not Alone

Look to the right and see;
For there is no one who regards me favorably;
There is no escape for me;
No one cares for my soul.
PSALM 142:4 NASB

As you wake up this morning, do you relate to these words at all? Life is a journey, and sometimes during this journey you look around you and wonder who is really by your side. Even if you have good relationships with family and friends around you, you can feel alone in your struggles and decisions.

Know today that you are not alone, for your good shepherd is guiding you all the way. Even though you feel as though you are in a valley, you are being led carefully through it. Jesus is right there, caring for your soul.

Jesus, my heart is overwhelmed with gratitude for showing me that you are by my side right now. I have felt so alone at times, yet I know you are near. When I feel at my lowest point, help me to see you next to me.

Free My Soul

Free me from my prison,
and then I will praise your name.
Then good people will surround me,
because you have taken care of me.
PSALM 142:7 NCV

Nobody likes the thought of being stuck in something they can't get out of. You don't have to have been in prison or trapped in an elevator to know what it would feel like to not be in control of your freedom. These days, we probably feel a little more like we are trapped in a job or mental illness, or maybe we are even trapped by our own sin.

The truth is that Jesus came to set you free. He does not want you to be in a prison of any description. When you ask for a breakthrough, expect freedom, and then be ready to encourage other believers with what he has done for you.

Jesus, free me from my prison! I will praise your name now, knowing that you will give me freedom.

Before Birth

You brought me out of the womb;
you made me trust in you,
even at my mother's breast.

PSALM 22:9 NIV

Jesus was the Word from the beginning—with God in the creation of this world and the creation of humanity. Jesus had a hand in creating you! It's great to know of Jesus as he was on earth, but it's also important to remember where and who he was from the beginning.

Jesus can not only empathize with you from a human perspective, but he also knows you inside out. Talk to him today as the person who knows you the best.

Jesus, thank you that you are a divine and human person and that you know me so well. As I go into my day, help me to recognize your Spirit speaking to me and working in me. I love you, my Savior and my friend.

Blessed with Provision

I have been young, and now am old;
yet I have not seen the righteous forsaken,
nor his descendants begging bread.
PSALM 37:25 NKJV

Your day might be looking a little grim with so many deadlines and things to get done. You might be wondering when you will get a day where you feel his blessing of time, peace, and fun!

Being a child of the Almighty gains you access to that blessed feeling every day even when your circumstances are ordinary or difficult. You are a child of the King, and his blessings are yours.

Jesus, thank you that your grace is there to pick me up today and give me a day where I can experience the fullness of your love and provision.

His Pasture

Then we your people, the sheep of your pasture,
will thank you forever and ever,
praising your greatness from generation to generation.
PSALM 79:13 NLT

In Jesus' day there were many shepherds. It is interesting that sheep learn their shepherd's voice and only follow the voice they know.

When you follow Jesus, you are both known by him and you know his voice. We know that a shepherd diligently watches over his sheep to keep them from harm. Jesus not only does that, but he also gave his life for us. He gave his life for you.

Jesus, you are my good shepherd. I feel blessed because I am known by you. Help me to know your voice more so I can follow closely in your footsteps and be safe from harm.

Healthy Trees

Like trees planted in the Temple of the LORD,
they will grow strong in the courtyards of our God.
PSALM 92:13 NCV

Take a moment to reflect on a time when you felt you were giving the best of yourself. You may be thinking of times when you were utilizing your gifts and talents and could witness your positive influence in others around you. You may not have to reflect back far, or you could be wondering where those times have gone!

Jesus describes himself as the vine. If we are being nourished from that source, we will produce fruit. In the times where we feel like we are not flourishing, it may be that the Father needs to do some necessary pruning—for the health of both the branch and the whole vine.

Heavenly Father, I ask you to show me areas of my life that you have chosen to prune. Help me to be encouraged that you have done this so I can be fruitful in other areas of my life.

Seventy or Eighty

Our days may come to seventy years,
or eighty, if our strength endures;
yet the best of them are but trouble and sorrow,
for they quickly pass, and we fly away.
PSALM 90:10 NIV

It doesn't matter what age you are; you are always headed toward getting older! That's not to make you feel depressed, but it is simply a truth that we all have to deal with whether we are close to seventy or not! If you aren't feeling down enough, you can add in that the best of your years are spent working hard and going through some pretty difficult things!

The psalms can be a welcome relief of the fears and despair we experience as humans. It is ok to lament; just remember that there is always hope and goodness to be found on the other side.

God, I don't want to get older! There is something about life that can make me feel burdened that we never quite get away from trouble and sorrow. Give me hope that you intended me to live this life abundantly despite the sorrow.

A Thousand Years

*A thousand years in your sight
are but as yesterday when it is past,
or as a watch in the night.*
PSALM 90:4 NCV

It's an interesting thought to consider that God's time and space could be different to ours. If you try to think too hard about how the Creator of our universe manages to understand and care for all his creation, you will find your mind trying to explain it in all kinds of ways. It's little wonder that we conclude he just sits so far above it, or outside of time, as others would put it.

Don't let this discourage you because we hold a very real truth that God is also very near and present to us. May your day hold this tension well between the God of the universe who is also the God of your heart.

God, I can't begin to understand how your intelligence filters into this world, but I know that I am blessed to be known and loved by you.

Sun Kissed

Fill us with your love every morning.
Then we will sing and rejoice all our lives.
PSALM 90:14 NCV

It's hard to admit, but sometimes the only thing that gets us up in the morning is the thought of coffee. If you're not a coffee lover, it might be breakfast that entices you to put your feet on the floor and drag yourself out of bed.

Imagine if we could experience the fullness of God's love every morning and be as eager to get up because of this wonderful assurance. It might take you a while to get into the habit of asking the Spirit of Christ to fill you up, but every time you do, you will know that he is near. Sing and rejoice today because he loves you.

Holy Spirit, I am grateful that you are able to fill me with your love. Please break through any resistance I might have to receiving your love.

Successful Efforts

May the favor of the LORD our God rest on us;
establish the work of our hands for us—
yes, establish the work of our hands.
PSALM 90:17 NIV

Chances are that you will have to work in some shape or form today. You might be heading out to your job, volunteering for a community project, or just cleaning up around the home. Sometimes our list of jobs and chores seems endless and we wonder why we are stuck in this routine of maintenance!

Be encouraged to ask God the same thing this writer asks of him— to turn your work into something meaningful. Don't ever feel like your work isn't for a purpose. In some way, working is either benefiting you, or those you love. Try to approach your work with joy today.

Lord, establish the work of my hands today. Give me a good attitude and a resilient mind and body to get through the day.

The Fair Judge

Say among the nations, "The LORD reigns.
The world is firmly established; it cannot be shaken.
He judges the peoples fairly."
PSALM 96:10 CSB

Our courts use judges to make rulings and decisions about important societal matters. A judge is relied upon to make sound conclusions according to their knowledge, expertise, and common sense. But no judge is perfect, which is why it should be a relief to understand God as the supreme ruler and judge of all.

God, in his perfect understanding, made this world and the creatures that live within it. He firmly established his creation, and he firmly establishes his Word among us. Be encouraged that you are governed by the only true, fair, and righteous judge.

Lord, I am blessed to know you as my Redeemer. Thank you that you don't see me as someone to punish, but as someone to love and restore.

Defining Moments

As for me, I shall behold Your face in righteousness;
I shall be satisfied with Your likeness when I awake.
PSALM 17:15 NASB

There are moments of life when we have time to reflect and sometimes those reflections bring us to a place of dissatisfaction. You might be feeling dissatisfied with your career or studies. You might even feel like you are going nowhere in your relationship or that you haven't been able to use your gifts or talents in the right environment.

What is the source of that dissatisfaction? Is it that you are holding up other people as a measure of where you want to be? Are you looking at the world's definition of what it means to make it in life? Be encouraged that what matters the most to your Creator is that you live a life that is fully you. He didn't create you to be anything other than yourself.

Jesus, my friend, thank you for showing me that I am fully accepted for who I am and what I have already done in this life. Help me to stop chasing my own ideas of success and give me contentment in knowing that I belong to you.

Anger Danger

Don't get angry.
Don't be upset;
it only leads to trouble.
PSALM 37:8 NCV

When was the last time you had a frustrating conversation with someone and felt like you got nowhere in your discussion? Sometimes we simply don't see eye-to-eye with people, and it's like talking in circles without really being able to land an understanding of each other's perspectives.

In times like this, you need to seek out the help of the Holy Spirit. He is the person who intimately understands everyone because he was there from inception. Try to turn your frustration into a prayer for that person and ask for the Holy Spirit to open your eyes and ears to the heart of the matter.

Holy Spirit, I will need help in my discussions with others today. Give me wisdom and discernment and a willingness to really try to understand someone else's perspective.

My Fortress

The LORD is my light and my salvation—
so why should I be afraid?
The LORD is my fortress,
protecting me from danger,
so why should I tremble?
PSALM 27:1 NLT

It's time to face another day, and even though you might not feel ready for it, God is already strengthening you with peace, wisdom, and hope. Remember that you can always count on him to equip you with what you need as you need it.

What do you need right now? Is it motivation to simply have a shower and get dressed? Is it peace to calm your anxious nerves about an exam at school? You might need a bit of patience as you try and chase your kids to get ready for school. Ask him for what you need—he cares about the small stuff and is more than ready to give you help.

Lord, I need your help right now and I will need your help throughout the day. I am grateful that your presence is with me through it all.

Lasting Love

Keep on giving your thanks to God,
for he is so good!
His constant, tender love lasts forever!
PSALM 118:1 TPT

There is something about news things that really get us excited. New babies, new houses, new jobs, new relationships…they are all incredibly exciting, but can also be very daunting because they carry with them the sense of the unknown.

Today is a new day, and it should be full of hope and promise, but there will also be unknowns throughout your day. There will be people you meet, there might be an unexpected phone call, or you might get detoured on the way home because of terrible traffic. Life is full of unknowns, but instead of worrying about all of those, let yourself delight in the fact that life is an adventure and it is exciting largely because you don't know it all!

God, I often feel excited and nervous at the same time. Remind me today that you are in control and I can allow myself to be content in all circumstances.

Digging Holes

Whoever digs a hole and scoops it out
falls into the pit they have made.
PSALM 7:15 NIV

Is there someone in your life right now that seems to be manipulating everyone in the wrong direction? There are people who are dishonest and selfish, but often these very people have such great charisma that nobody seems to see through the façade to the real person. Smooth talkers and those who present themselves as successful easily fool us.

Instead of trying to convince others that they are manipulative, sit back and let the consequences take care of themselves. Take some comfort in this verse. Life has a way of sorting the foolish and the wise.

Lord, I don't wish harm on people who are living a selfish life, but I am thankful that your light and love will be the truth that prevails in this sometimes very foolish world.

Breathing Life

Let everything that has breath
praise the LORD.
Praise the LORD.
PSALM 150:6 NIV

Exercise classes are a pretty big thing these days. You might even be planning on going to one this morning or later this day. Some classes are high-intensity aerobic and others are slower with greater demand on your muscles. Although there are a variety of ways you can exercise, there is one thing that is always a focus, and this is your breathing!

Experts say that the way you breathe through an exercise can make all of the difference. Breathing is part of living, and it is part of living well. Focus on your breath in this moment and be grateful that you serve the God who gave it to you.

God, I am grateful for each breath that I take right now because it is you who gave me life. I choose to appreciate this life, and praise you for making me.

Even in Bed

Let those who worship him
rejoice in his glory.
Let them sing for joy even in bed!
PSALM 149:5 NCV

The Israelites would often have very arduous rituals to seek out the presence of God. What a joy it must have been to know that God could be praised from one's own bed!

You may have gotten out of bed already, but take some time to appreciate that you can approach your loving King in the comfort of your own room. Jesus has made a way to make his home in your heart, so be mindful of his presence within you today.

Holy Spirit, I am delighted to have you with me in everything that I do. I worship you and rejoice in your glory.

World Masters

You made them rulers over the works of your hands;
you put everything under their feet.
PSALM 8:6 NIV

God's creation is beautiful and astounding, but he put extra special effort into making humanity. Not only are we created with beauty and intricacy, but we also have been given the status of being special because we are the ones that have been made in God's image.

Every part of nature reveals something of God, and we are the pinnacle of this revelation displayed perfectly through Jesus. If you are feeling insignificant or weak this morning, remind yourself that God has chosen to show himself through you. Now that is a significant job!

Father, thank you for choosing to reveal yourself through me. Help me to be bold in my faith today, knowing that you have created me with this important purpose in mind.

Jaws

Be gracious to me, LORD;
consider my affliction at the hands of those who hate me.
Lift me up from the gates of death.
PSALM 9:13 CSB

Some days you just feel like the world is against you. Maybe you ran out of coffee or hot water for your shower. The weather might have turned bad just before you went out for your morning walk. You might have ended up yelling at your family and everyone left the house mad.

Each thing that goes wrong seems to add a little more salt to the wound. This is where you need the healing power of God's grace to soothe the pain of emotional and mental affliction. Call out to him this morning and watch him pull you safely away from the angry jaws of despair.

Be gracious to me, O Lord. See my pain and encourage my heart before things get worse. Thank you that you will always come to my rescue.

So Far Away

Why, O LORD, do you stand far away?
Why do you hide yourself in times of trouble?
PSALM 10:1 ESV

What do you do when you feel like God is not there for you anymore? There are times when you seem to be asking God for the answers to a difficult situation and you just don't feel like you can hear him. The Scriptures are full of saying that God is near, yet you just don't seem to feel his presence anymore.

These moments can sometimes be described as our wilderness times when we feel like God has abandoned us. But just like the Israelites in the wilderness, God was there, taking care of their needs and watching over them. If you are feeling an absence of God's presence this morning, express it to him and try to be aware of how he is providing for you—whether you feel it or not.

Lord, why do you stand far away? Why do you hide yourself in times of trouble? Be near to me today. I need you.

Pray and Do

Arise, LORD!
Lift up your hand, O God.
Do not forget the helpless.
PSALM 10:12 NIV

When you are driving around a school zone, you might see crossing wardens who put up their hand to stop you from driving while children are crossing. There is so much trouble and injustice in this world that sometimes we just want God to raise his hand and put a stop to it all. Why doesn't this good God prevent things from happening?

It's ok to ask these questions because every day we have to sit with the tension that God is good and yet there are still evil things happening in the world around us. Instead of questioning God's goodness, we can pray the prayer of the psalmist—that we would see an end to all the wrong in this life.

Life up your hand, O God. Do not forget the helpless.

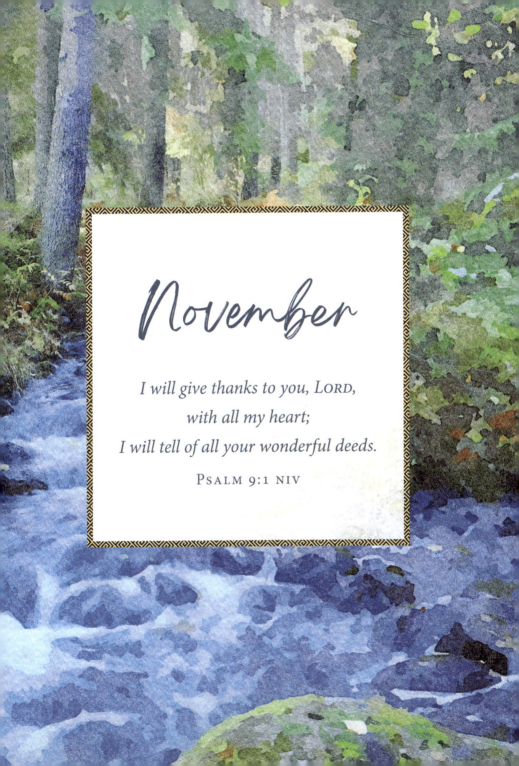

November

I will give thanks to you, Lord,
with all my heart;
I will tell of all your wonderful deeds.

PSALM 9:1 NIV

Calm Being

You open your hand;
you satisfy the desire of every living thing.
PSALM 145:16 ESV

If you are a cat lover, you will know the calm it can bring as you feel its warm body snuggled up next to you gently purring. If it's not cats that you are into, perhaps you are soothed by the sound of gentle rain on the roof. There are things that God can use in nature to calm and soothe our emotions.

Before you head into a day that will be full of noise and possibly a bit of stress, seek out that thing or place that gives you peace and calms your soul. Use the gifts within this world that God has given for you to use for your wellbeing.

Heavenly Father, thank you for the gift of your creation that can bring me relief in the middle of trouble. Help me to pay attention to things that bring me peace so I can approach each day with the right frame of mind.

What to Do

If the foundations are destroyed,
what can the righteous do?
PSALM 11:3 ESV

Often we try our very hardest and still don't get the outcome that we were hoping for. You might try to make a right decision in your workplace, yet the project still falls apart. You might think you have dealt fairly with your children, but they still grumble and complain. Perhaps you followed the rulebook on the right diet and still don't feel any healthier.

What do the righteous do when the foundations of what should work, doesn't? You might never get your answer but pray that you find peace in the knowledge that the mystery of God's ways will one day be revealed.

Lord, I have become exasperated at times because I simply can't understand why things don't work together in the way they should. Help me to fix my thoughts on what is right and to submit to your transcendent wisdom.

Second Opinion

When you appear, I worship
while all of my enemies run in retreat.
They stumble and perish before your presence.
PSALM 9:3 TPT

When you go to the doctor about a condition that needs explaining, you might not always be confident in their diagnosis. People will usually encourage you to get a second opinion. There are times when significant people in your life have told you something about yourself that makes you feel terrible. They might have labelled you as selfish, or crazy, or any number of accusations.

This is your time to get a second opinion, so go straight to your heavenly Father and ask him what he thinks. This is your God, who created you and loves you unconditionally and sees nothing but the best, redeemed person that you are.

Lord, thank you that when you appear, it is right by my side. Help my accusers to be put to shame when you show up to cover me.

Humble Road

He leads the humble in what is right,
and teaches the humble his way.
PSALM 25:9 ESV

Jesus showed just how great his love was by doing the job that was reserved for a lowly servant. He was revered by his disciples as a great teacher, yet he gladly showed the disciples his affection through an act of humility.

Jesus wants us to show this same humility for one another. It doesn't matter if we have a higher position, career, or place in society, we need Jesus' heart of compassion to serve one another in love.

Jesus, thank you for showing me humility. You have such great love for all people and I want to honor your words that tell me to do what you have done. As I go into the busyness of life today, I ask that your Holy Spirit gives me the grace to love as you do.

Miraculous

You are the God who does miracles;
you have shown people your power.
PSALM 77:14 NCV

The Bible is full of exciting accounts of power, healing, and resurrection. We find ourselves wishing that we had been there when the fire of God fell upon Elijah's sacrifice, or when Lazarus stepped out of the tomb.

God is clear that miracles didn't stop when the Bible ended. His power isn't limited by the ages, and he is just as omnipotent today as he always has been. Approach this day with hope in your heart.

Lord, give me faith again to believe in the miracles that you did in the Bible and to believe that you can do miracles today.

Sheltered

The LORD is your protector;
The LORD is your shade on your right hand.
PSALM 121:5 NASB

Jesus knew that the disciples couldn't keep his commandments without help. Israel hadn't been able to prove their faithfulness, and neither can we. That's why part of the wonderful plan of salvation included the Holy Spirit who would teach us Jesus' ways until he returns.

The Holy Spirit is within you, to guide you in truth and to continue to teach you the ways of Christ.

Holy Spirit, thank you for helping me to keep the commandments of our faith. Thank you for the grace to get through each day. Allow me to be aware of your presence within me today.

Shout for Joy

May we shout for joy when we hear of your victory
and raise a victory banner in the name of our God.
May the LORD answer all your prayers.
PSALM 20:5 NLT

We often pray without expecting much of a response, so it is good to acknowledge those times when we see that God has answered our prayers.

These stories in Scripture help to build our faith and so do the stories of our answered prayers. They are there to be shared. Be encouraged today to continue to present your requests to God, knowing that he is listening.

Father God, I have many prayers and petitions, some of them answered, others not. I am encouraged that you do answer prayers, understanding that sometimes it is not the answer I want. Let me continue to remember and share those stories where I have witnessed your answers and let these stories encourage those who hear them.

Keep Your Distance

Though the LORD is great,
he cares for the humble,
but he keeps his distance from the proud.
PSALM 138:6 NLT

It's a competitive world and we are prone to falling into the trap of making ourselves appear better than others or make our stories seem bigger than they really are. We talk about our strengths, skills, jobs, and victories a lot more than we talk of our failures. We post our glory moments to social media and often leave out the junk.

God wants you to celebrate the good things in your life, but measure your motivation for sharing your wins. Make sure that you are not speaking from a heart of arrogance. God cares not about what you say but from the heart in which you conduct yourself.

Lord, help me not to compare myself to others. Forgive me when I have boasted in order to look better than others. Help me to lift others up today and be a positive influence in the lives of those people that I encounter.

Break the Pride

The sacrifice God wants is a broken spirit.
God, you will not reject a heart
that is broken and sorry for sin.
PSALM 51:17 NCV

When you have been wronged and somebody offers up a simple, "Sorry," it doesn't feel like a true apology if they continue to wrong you. Sometimes saying the right thing or going through the right formalities isn't enough to show love.

God didn't want Israel's sacrifice's just for the sake of ritual; he wanted their obedience because that would mean that they understood why he wanted them to keep his commandments. Love God and love others. This is what God is calling you to do today.

Lord, I am sorry when I have paid lip service to Christian morality. I know that you desire my heart and not just my religious actions. Teach me to respond in my heart to your call to love you and love others.

Chosen for Integrity

Lord, defend me because I have lived an innocent life.
I have trusted the Lord and never doubted.
Psalm 26:1 NCV

It is uplifting to read that God doesn't judge by outward appearances, but it can be a challenge to imitate God in this respect. Jesse thought his eldest looked the part of a king and yet it was David, the youngest with a good heart, whom God chose.

While we don't always know someone's heart, we ought to give people the benefit of not judging them by what we first see or hear from them. We cross a lot of new people in one day. Perhaps you can see people from a different perspective today.

Lord, thank you that you care more about the heart of a person than what is displayed on the outside. Help me to approach people with this same consideration, and to see beyond the surface.

In Your Hand

Let them praise the LORD,
because they were created by his command.
PSALM 148:5 NCV

God wants to use you in so many different ways, be it in your daily life or in a specific mission that he sets out for you. God doesn't, however, want you to try and be like somebody else in the way that you approach things. You don't have to talk like a famous preacher or lead a Bible study like your friend. You don't have to sing in the band to be influential.

God needs you to be you! He wants you to wear the things that make you who you are in order to do his work. David couldn't wear Saul's armor; he just needed his everyday attire to get the job done. Wear your own shoes as you walk into today's tasks and be proud of them.

God, thank you for giving me a specific personality, set of experiences, style, and opportunities that are uniquely mine. Help me to be comfortable with the person I have become and to use my unique self to accomplish your will.

Still Working

The LORD will fulfill his purpose for me;
your steadfast love, O LORD, endures forever.
Do not forsake the work of your hands.
PSALM 138:8 ESV

We can be impatient at times especially when we have held onto hope for a long time. The Israelites were desperate to be released from their oppression; they wanted to experience victory in their nation.

You might have hopes for a relationship to be restored, for a family member to receive salvation, to have a child, or to get a promotion. It isn't God's nature to tell us exactly how things are going to turn out, but he does assure us that we will have the power of the Holy Spirit and we can trust that God will still work in our circumstances.

Holy Spirit, thank you that you are with me. Let me become more aware of your presence so I will be assured that you are still working powerfully in my circumstances. I hold onto the hope that you will bring my hopes to fulfilment.

Crucified for You

I am a worm and not a man,
scorned by mankind and despised by the people.
PSALM 22:6 ESV

It's hard to imagine that after all of Jesus' miracles and teaching, people still wanted to crucify him. He didn't come in violence or arrogance, yet he was still despised by many.

Despite all the rejection, Jesus was victorious. Be encouraged if you are facing challenges today that while people may reject you for no good reason, you can be victorious. Stand tall and be proud of who you are in Christ.

Jesus, thank you for reminding me that you understand rejection. Help me in my low points during the day to take courage that my confidence comes from you and not others.

Intervention

Defend the weak and the orphans;
defend the rights of the poor and suffering.
PSALM 82:3 NCV

If you have spent enough time around children, you will know that sometimes the fighting between siblings seems endless and is often pointless!

We all recognize that fighting rarely gets us what we want, yet we still enter into arguments and disputes, rarely considering the consequence. As you prepare to talk, plan, and work with people today, remember that peace is better than the sword.

Lord, thank you for giving me opportunities to work and discuss things with people. Help me to conduct these discussions today with peace and grace in all circumstances.

The Present

*You have commanded us
to keep Your precepts diligently.*
PSALM 119:4 NKJV

Have you woken up this morning worrying about the jobs you
have to get through or if you will have enough time to get to the
things that you really want to do, like going to the gym or catching
up with that friend at lunchtime?

When you begin to get so busy you are always concerned about
what is next, yet sometimes God just wants you to be present in the
moment and make the best of what is in your hands or heart right
now. Take some time to think about the present needs, either of
yourself or someone else, and let God take care of the next thing.

Jesus, help me to still my heart and mind this morning and to be
able to be present with the people and tasks that are set before me.
Help me to be able to focus on one thing at a time.

Bedrock

The LORD is my rock, my protection, my Savior.
My God is my rock.
I can run to him for safety.
He is my shield and my saving strength, my defender.
PSALM 18:2 NCV

Have you had those times when you are feeling down but don't exactly know why? There are so many reasons you might be feeling a little off: physical health, hormones, or that social disconnection where you just aren't sure anyone really understands where your heart and head are.

In those times of feeling a bit disoriented, remember that life is a process and if we didn't feel this way at times, there would be nothing to work through and discover at the end. All hard work ends in some kind of fruit, so dig your heels in and work through your discouragement.

Lord, thank you for not requiring me to be happy all the time but to diligently seek you so you can help me work through the way that I am feeling. Give me some perspective and wisdom as I work through what is going on in my heart.

Onwards

This God is our God for ever and ever;
he will be our guide even to the end.
PSALM 48:14 NIV

Life gets a little bit harder year by year. As children, we don't seem to have many cares, and then we are thrown into the world of responsibility. Along with that comes stress and heartache.

Even if you haven't experienced a misfortune, you are likely to know someone who has, and in those times it is really hard to know what to do or say. Sometimes all we can do is acknowledge that life is hard. Today, set aside a few minutes to pray for people who are hurting or in some kind of dilemma. Pray that God would be able to give them a measure of peace and hope during this time.

Lord, I am grateful that you will always be the light in the darkness that can lead me through any circumstance. Please be that light for my friends who are struggling today.

Listen to Me

Come, children of God, and listen to me.
I'll share the lesson I've learned of fearing the LORD.
PSALM 34:11 TPT

Is there ever a good time to share your faith lessons with friends? We never quite know when we should be gracious and respect people's journey, or when God might be using us to provide someone with some wisdom.

If you are feeling caught between knowing when to speak and when not to speak, make sure to be in constant prayer. When you are seeking the guidance of Jesus, his Holy Spirit will be right there with the words, or with the silence! Most importantly, remember that being a good friend means to be Jesus to that person—so make sure you ask yourself how Jesus would treat others and do the same.

Jesus, thank you that you were a person of peace, grace, and love. Thank you that you always look at a person's heart and not their actions. Give me the wisdom to know when I can help someone with words or just with love.

Bubble Wrap

Because he holds fast to me in love,
I will deliver him;
I will protect him,
because he knows my name.
PSALM 91:14 ESV

We don't like when things break. It might be your favorite coffee mug, a car part, or even a fingernail. When things are broken, it can involve an emotional loss of something you were connected to, or a financial loss, or it might just be a superficial but irritating loss of appearance (like that hand that now has uneven nails).

Brokenness is part of our human experience, yet we wish it wasn't. There is a desire for things to stay whole. Thank the Lord this morning that brokenness is temporary, and our God will one day make all things new again.

Jesus, I can get so upset about all the brokenness around me. Thank you for giving me a sense that things are not right when they are broken because it reminds me that your kingdom is here but still yet to come.

Sideline

The LORD of Heaven's Armies is here among us;
the God of Israel is our fortress.
PSALM 46:7 NLT

When you are watching your favorite sports team play, you remain completely invested in what is happening with each player and move. Everyone on the other team, whether player or spectator, feels like the enemy. It's good to be part of a team and to cheer people on even when you are on the sideline.

The next time you feel like someone in your community, friendship circle, or family is starting to have a difficult time, make sure that you spend some time investing in cheering them on and encouraging them to pick themselves up and keep going.

Holy Spirit, thank you for the gift of community. Lead me toward the people in my community that are in need of some encouragement and give me the words and actions that I need to be able to cheer these people on.

Mourning

You keep track of all my sorrows.
You have collected all my tears in your bottle.
You have recorded each one in your book.
PSALM 56:8 NLT

The relationship of David and Jonathan is known for being a deep friendship, closer than brothers. It is fitting that when Jonathan dies in battle, David writes and mourns for him.

It is often said that the greater the love, the greater the grief. You may have experienced the loss of a loved one or know of someone who has. It is important that we are able to express this grief, remembering that God is our great comforter.

Lord, today I remember those whom I have loved and lost. I pray that you would help me to express my grief in a way that is healing and recognizes your comfort. Thank you that you care for my heart.

Ark of Strength

Rise up, Lord, come to your resting place,
you and your powerful ark.
PSALM 132:8 CSB

David was a keen worshipper, but he also had a great reason to dance! The ark of the covenant was back in his possession and having the Lord's presence with him meant that God's favor was with David and his kingdom. He had a huge reason to celebrate.

You have a reason to celebrate too. The presence of God is with you—he is in your heart—and that means his favor is with you. Dance before the Lord like no one is watching today!

God, thank you for sending your Son, Jesus, who made a way for your presence to live inside of me. Bring me the joy of knowing that I have your strength, power, and grace within me and give me an extra spring in my step as I go about my day.

The Greatest Leader

Our God is in heaven;
he does whatever pleases him.
PSALM 115:3 NIV

It is good to remember and acknowledge that God is sovereign. This world has kings, rulers, presidents, and many leaders, but none are as great as our God. He is the everlasting King and he is the one that makes promises that are enduring and true.

Remind yourself today as you go into a world full of different systems and beliefs that God is truth and he will continue to be good toward you, his faithful servant.

God, you are sovereign, and you are my Lord. Thank you for showing me favor despite a world that has shown me hardship. Thank you that I can lift my eyes above the things of the world to see your ways as the truth. I honor you today and ask that your truth would shine through me.

Equipped

You equipped me with strength for the battle;
you made those who rise against me sink under me.
PSALM 18:39 ESV

Christians speak of peace, love, and grace, but there are times when we have to fight for our faith. It isn't usually a physical battle, but can be a battle of the mind, heart, emotions, or will. We need other Christians in this life to help us in our battles.

Sometimes the battle is too strong for a friend, and we have to come to the rescue. At times, the battle will be too hard for us and we will need to call on our friends for help. As you prepare for the day ahead, be ready with God's armor for whatever may come your way.

Lord, thank you for friends that are willing to come to my rescue in times of need. I pray you would help me to be attentive to the troubles that others may be having and to stand alongside them and help them fight.

Play Well

Sing to Him a new song;
Play skillfully with a shout of joy.
PSALM 33:3 NKJV

The clean slate of a new day is filled with an air of expectation. It's like deep down inside there is something built into our heart and mind that longs to start afresh. This morning is the chance for you to start again. You may have had a bad day yesterday or felt like you didn't complete what you needed to, but today is a new and different day!

Whether you are a goal setter or someone who approaches the day with a whatever-may-come attitude, you have God's mercy and grace to help you achieve it.

Lord, thank you for letting me start new today and every day. I pray for faith to see what you have already begun.

He Forgives

Keep me from the sins of pride;
don't let them rule me.
Then I can be pure and innocent
of the greatest of sins.
PSALM 19:13 NCV

When Jesus hung on the cross, there were two thieves hanging beside him. One of those thieves, as he hung in his final moments of life, asked Jesus for grace and a second chance. That thief—minutes before death—was given forgiveness and eternal life. The very same day he entered paradise as a forgiven and clean man.

In light of his story, how can we ever say that it's too late to turn it all around?

Give me a fresh start today, Lord. I need to remember that your mercy and forgiveness awaits me every single morning. I trust in that forgiveness today and ask for a renewed sense of purpose for today.

For All

Surely his salvation is near to those who fear him,
so our land will be filled with his glory.
PSALM 85:9 NLT

Jesus didn't confine his ministry to the Jewish people and believers of his day. He extended his ministry to the Gentiles and everyone outside the law of the Scribes and the Pharisees.

You are included in God's great plan to extend salvation to the ends of the earth, so all nations come back to him. As you go into your community today, remember the great commission that God has given all of us.

Jesus, thank you that I have been included in the great big family of God. I have seen the light and now I want others to see that light too. I pray that the church would rise up and share your glory to the ends of the earth. Your kingdom come!

Rebuilding

The Lord will rebuild Jerusalem;
there his glory will be seen.
Psalm 102:16 ncv

You will have a lot of thoughts about your day ahead—grocery lists, medical appointments, sports training, or where you put those keys! We are so consumed with our thoughts of all of the details of the day ahead that we forget to think on the greatness of God.

When we allow our thoughts of God to take over, we see our small concerns about the day fall away. Ask God to break through your stresses and help you concentrate on what matters the most today.

Father God, thank you that in those times of deepest need you are the water of life that I can draw my strength from. Help me to drink of your living water today.

Losing Courage

The ships were tossed as high as the sky
and fell low to the depths.
The storm was so bad that they lost their courage.
PSALM 107:26 NCV

Sometimes it feels like life is tossing you around. Remember that it is not your circumstances that determine your anxiety; it is your faith. Pray for wisdom! But when you do, make sure you are ready to receive it.

Believe the word that the Lord has for you, and do not doubt. If you get stuck on a task or decision today, ask for God's wisdom. He promises to give it to you and to give liberally!

Jesus, thank you that I can have faith in your love and care for me in the middle of life's storms. Keep my heart steady and peaceful today.

Listen Up

Listen, both great and small,
rich and poor together.
PSALM 49:2 NCV

For some, listening comes naturally; for others, it is something that has to be worked on. There is an art to listening especially when you are upset.

If this happens today, be intentional about being slow to speak. Take time to think through what others are saying to you. Try to understand where they are coming from. Discern if they just need to talk. Wait for them to ask your opinion and consider if your response will be helpful.

Lord, help me to take the time to listen to others today. Help me to try to understand the heart of the matter and give me the grace to keep the peace.

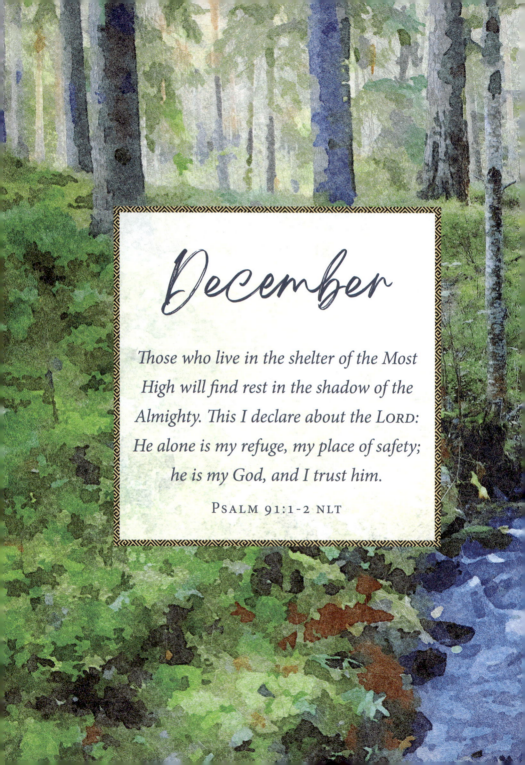

December

Those who live in the shelter of the Most High will find rest in the shadow of the Almighty. This I declare about the LORD: He alone is my refuge, my place of safety; he is my God, and I trust him.

PSALM 91:1-2 NLT

Love and Truth

Your kingdom is built on what is right and fair.
Love and truth are in all you do.
PSALM 89:14 NCV

What is your faith worth? How far are you willing to go to express the love of God to a dying world? Will you give of yourself when it isn't convenient? Will you love someone who seems unlovable and give to someone who can never repay you?

The cost may seem great and the work insignificant, but God sees your heart and what you have done, and he counts it as work done directly for him.

Lord, let me show my faith in action toward those in need. Holy Spirit, guide me to the needs of others whether it is someone close to me or needs of people in another country. Help me to respond quickly to help others.

Mouth of Arrows

They sharpen their tongues like swords
and aim cruel words like deadly arrows.
PSALM 64:3 NIV

It doesn't take long to realize the power of the tongue. Words can be our strongest device. There is no doubt that we are good at talking; the question is, do we talk good?

Who will you be talking to today? Can you exercise self-control when trying to organize your family? Can you show restraint when you get upset with a colleague? Can you steer your words away from gossip or untruth?

Heavenly Father, thank you for giving me the gift of communication. Help me to use my words for good and not for harm today.

Broken Promises

The one who was my friend
attacks his friends and breaks his promises.
PSALM 55:20 NCV

Quarrelling is as common for adults as it is for children; it just looks different in action. The heart behind fighting is the same, and the reactions stem from the same provocation. We have an internal war going on of selfish motives; we want to rise to the top and when we feel the need to fight for our pride, we quarrel until we feel we have won.

If you run into an argument today, examine your heart motive for fighting back and resist the urge to let pride get in the way.

Jesus, I don't like fighting with others, but sometimes I get so angry and frustrated that I do and say things that I don't intend to. Give me the strength to gain control over wrong things that might come into my heart and keep me from wrong actions today.

Crowned Victory

The Lord takes delight in his people;
he crowns the humble with victory.
Psalm 149:4 niv

Some of the most substantial and ultimately wonderful changes in our lives come from moments of vulnerability. But vulnerability takes one key ingredient: humility. And humility is not easy.

Isn't it sometimes easier for us to pretend that conflict never happened than to face the fact that we made a mistake and wronged another person? It's not always easy to humble ourselves and fight for the resolution
in an argument—especially when it means admitting our failures.

Jesus, show me grace for people in my life who have wronged me. In the same way, help me to be humble when I have wronged others, and prompt me to be quick to apologize when I am wrong.

Emerging

LORD, you give light to my lamp.
My God brightens the darkness around me.
PSALM 18:28 NCV

Do you ever feel like you can't feel God? Like you've lost sight of him somehow? Sometimes we aren't sure how to get back to that place where we feel his presence strongly and hear his voice clearly.

God will not push himself on you. He will not share his glory with another, and he will not try to compete with the world for your heart. But if you draw near to him, he will wrap you in the power of his presence. Welcome him into your life today.

Lord, be close to me today. There have been times where I don't know where you are or what you are doing, but I recognize that those are probably the times when I am not drawing close to you. Let me feel your presence surround me in all that I do today.

Changing Seasons

He made the moon to mark the seasons;
the sun knows its time for setting.
PSALM 104:19 ESV

You will, undoubtedly, have various seasons in your life: seasons of longing and contentment, seasons of discouragement and joy, seasons of more and less. Being a grown-up means stretching into new ways of living, and this usually doesn't happen until the season hits.

Don't make excuses for why you can't do what God is calling you to do. Be brave! God will not move you into something without giving you the grace you need to make it through.

Lord, thank you for the calling you have placed on my life. Please give me the courage to know that you are with me now as you may call me forward.

Palm Trees

The righteous flourish like the palm tree
and grow like a cedar in Lebanon.
PSALM 92:12 ESV

If you live in a cooler climate, you've probably experienced the gorgeous season that is fall. Each year, the leaves slowly turn to shades of golden yellow, orange, and red. It's a thing of beauty, but eventually, the leaves wither and die, then fall to the ground.

All too often, the same can happen with our relationship with the Lord. We get that initial fire for him; we burn brightly with it but lose our way and fall away from him. If we keep our trust in him, he tells us that our spiritual leaves will never wither. He wants our lives to be like trees that continually bear fruit.

Lord, I want to burn forever bright for you. Help me to stand up to the heat and the wind if that's what faces me today. Give me the assurance that I won't fall.

Wounded

Your arrows have wounded me,
and your hand has come down on me.
PSALM 38:2 NCV

Examine your scars and recall the wounds that gave them to
you. Depending on the severity of the injury, and how long ago
it occurred, running a finger along the scar may bring back vivid
memories of the pain you felt. You are healed, but also changed.

It may be painful, but explore your old heart wounds—the ones
that never seem to entirely heal. Begin the process of releasing
them to God and claim the promise of his true healing.

Lord, I have hurt in my life. I'm thankful that you have healed me,
but sometimes remembering the hurt brings the pain back. Please
remind me that I was saved from hurt and help me to dwell on
your healing.

Eternal Companion

It is you, a person like me,
my companion and good friend.
PSALM 55:13 NCV

It's easy to go about our day crossing our many to-do items off our lists and making sure we accomplish all our tasks. Sometimes, spending time with the Lord can become just another box to check off. Toilets? Cleaned. Groceries? Purchased. Scripture reading? Done.

Are you holding back in your relationship with the Lord, or have you given him all of your heart? Don't reserve anything. Give all of yourself to him! Seek him in all areas of your life. He is there wherever you look, waiting for you, wanting to connect with you.

Lord, I desire a real relationship with you. Let me seek you with all my heart so I can find you. Thank you that you are always near.

Understand Commands

I run in the path of your commands,
for you have broadened my understanding.
PSALM 119:32 NIV

What does it mean to covet your neighbor's things? In the times of the Bible, the number of livestock that a neighbor owned showed their wealth. We aren't that different today! We may not admit when we are jealous of what other people have, but we certainly know the things that we want that we do not yet have!

Instead of coveting sheep or goats, it might be your friend's house, car, clothes or job. It is a real challenge to be content with what you have when the world tries to sell you the idea that more is better. Try to avoid the temptation to want what other people have today and learn the habit of contentment.

God, help me to be aware of my heart attitude; forgive me and give me a feeling of peace and thankfulness with what I do have.

Light of Your Face

It was not by their sword that they won the land,
nor did their arm bring them victory;
it was your right hand, your arm,
and the light of your face,
for you loved them.
PSALM 44:3 NIV

Have you ever been to a country where the light shines all the way through the night? It is a strange sensation to be able to go outside as if it is day and yet it is actually midnight!

It will indeed be a unique day when Jesus returns, but it isn't something to fear; it is something to look forward to. As you go through your day, watching the temperature get warmer and the sky get darker, remember the hope you have for your eternal future.

Lord, I marvel at what the day is going to be like when you return once again. I know I cannot even begin to imagine the beauty of your light, but I thank you for a glimpse into the beauty of that day.

Rebels and Rescue

Again and again he rescued them,
but they chose to rebel against him,
and they were finally destroyed by their sin.
Psalm 106:43 NLT

We see the wrestling match between God's mercy and love throughout the Old Testament. God calls his people to turn back to him and do it his way, they disobey, and they are punished. Yet, so many times, God turns from punishing to protecting. His heart was always to bless his people, not destroy them.

If you are wondering whether God is trying to punish you for something, remember this Scripture. He is determined to rescue you even when you rebel.

God, sometimes I feel like you should be angry with me for all my selfish ways. Thank you for your astounding love that leads you to be merciful to me. Help this love to get rid of any fear that is in my heart.

At Home

The one thing I ask of the Lord—
the thing I seek most—
is to live in the house of the Lord
all the days of my life,
delighting in the Lord's perfections
and meditating in his Temple.

PSALM 27:4 NLT

It is a scene that is played out in movies, books, and even in our imaginations. People sitting together, talking, and enjoying one another's company. Children playing games in the streets, completely safe, laughing and relishing the freedom of life.

These ideals are exactly how God wants us to view his kingdom. He wants us to know that one day there will be conversations, peace, fun, laughter, and connectedness. Allow yourself to dream a little as you prepare yourself for the day.

Lord, thank you for giving me a beautiful picture to start my day. Thank you that I see glimpses of your kingdom happening even now. I pray I would see the fullness of that kingdom soon.

Good Hearts

God protects me like a shield;
he saves those whose hearts are right.
PSALM 7:10 NCV

We can go through all the right Christian expectations—going to church, fasting, tithing, serving on the music or children's team. We can help out with missions and take communion or recite liturgy. All of these are excellent Christian disciplines, but we need to examine our heart motivations for why we are doing them.

If you seek these things for praise from others, or because it somehow fills your expectations, then they aren't worth a whole lot to God. He wants you to be motivated to do things for him because you love just as he does.

God, as I go into my day, I pray you would help me to examine my heart and why I am doing the various things I do. Give me the same love that you have for others so my actions truly come from my heart.

Skillful Poet

Beautiful words stir my heart.
I will recite a lovely poem about the king,
for my tongue is like the pen of a skillful poet.
PSALM 45:1 NLT

Have you ever wandered through an art gallery and wondered why you weren't given the kind of talent that many of the artists have? You might be someone lucky enough to have been blessed with the gift of drawing or painting, but it certainly isn't for everyone.

Instead of feeling envious of someone else's gift and talents, learn to appreciate the beauty that can be created by others. You might not be able to paint, but you might sing or be extraordinarily organized. Learn to appreciate the beauty of your own gifts, even if they don't seem as glorious as others. What you have to offer this world is unique and wonderful, so get started with your day being pleased that God made you just to be you!

Creator God, give me a contentment and pleasure in expressing the gifts that you have given me. Let me use these gifts for your glory, so others can appreciate your beauty through me.

Hunger Pangs

By the power of your hand, O Lord,
destroy those who look to this world for their reward.
But satisfy the hunger of your treasured ones.
May their children have plenty,
leaving an inheritance for their descendants.
PSALM 17:14 NLT

What will you have for breakfast this morning? Do you wake up hungry and ready for a big start to the day, or does your appetite grow as the day goes on? The Bible often compares our hunger for food to the way we hunger for God. There is a difference in our actions and attitudes when we are hungry and when we are being fed. The thoughts of a hungry person will be almost solely focused on what they are going to eat next. They are eager to get to that food.

Wouldn't it be good if you could hunger for the things of God in the same way? Try to focus your thoughts on Jesus today as though your life depended on it.

Jesus, help me to be aware of your presence today. When I notice that I haven't experienced you, help me to center my thoughts back on you.

Make the Best

How joyful are those who fear the Lord—
all who follow his ways!
PSALM 128:1 NLT

You have probably been in the position of deciding to move on, whether it's from a house, a job, or even a relationship. There is grief associated with leaving behind something that you have been so familiar with: things that have been a part of your life for years and have shaped who you are as a person or as a family. But life is full of changes and we can choose to face the next step with fear or with courage.

If you are feeling apprehensive about the next big step in your life, remember that you are not alone. Trust that God is helping you to create new memories, a new journey, and new opportunities to build your faith.

Lord, I feel quite nervous about what is ahead for me. Sometimes I worry that I have made a wrong decision about leaving and I don't know how to take the next step forward. Give me courage as I trust in you today.

Soda Pop

Praise the LORD, for the LORD is good;
celebrate his lovely name with music.
PSALM 135:3 NLT

When you get up in the morning you might have high aspirations for your day ahead. You might feel like a can of soda that fizzes and pops the moment it is opened. Take advantage of the times when you feel this way and use it as an opportunity to get things done!

You might feel energized enough to go for a brisk walk outside, put a few loads of washing on, write in your journal, or make breakfast for your household. You know all too well what happens if you leave that soda open for too long. Eventually the fizz will die down and the drink will become flat. So, get out there and make hay while the sun shines!

God, thank you for those days when I have enough energy to motivate me to do things that I really want to get done. Thank you for the gift of my body that can be used to be productive.

Raw Emotions

Charge them with crime upon crime;
do not let them share in your salvation.
PSALM 69:27 NIV

Are we allowed to wish the worst on those people that we consider enemies? It seems like a lot of the psalms assume that God is on our side and ready to defeat all the people we don't like, yet this seems a bit like asking God to let our home team win a sports game!

It's important to remember that many of the psalms are there to give expression to our emotions—even those that seem so extreme. When you read some of these words, you might feel offended at the language and lack of grace expressed in them. If we let people read our thoughts, we might just realize that those same expressions exist in us.

Jesus, I am glad that you allow us to be real and to share our thoughts and feelings even if they seem ugly and lack grace. Help me to be able to express how I feel to you, knowing that you can take my words and do what you know is right to do with them.

Promised Pursuit

*God could never forget his holy promise
to his servant Abraham.*
PSALM 105:42 TPT

God never gave up on his people. Though they forgot him and scattered to other lands and served other gods, he pursued them with all his heart.

If you have woken up this morning wondering if God wants to be near you, trust in the truth of his heart which is shown so clearly in his Word. He is pursuing your heart and will not stop until you accept his love. Sing and rejoice. He is coming for you.

Heavenly Father, thank you for pursuing me until I have no choice but to surrender to the wonder of your love. Give me a day full of the knowledge that you want to surround me with your presence.

Cost of Living

Truly, no ransom avails for one's life,
there is no price one can give to God for it.
PSALM 49:7 NRSV

The economy of God runs a whole lot different than our world systems. It should be that when you gather enough money for yourself then you will be satisfied with a great house, plenty of clothes, and glorious food! This is the falsity of the world: that money is what offers you comfort and prosperity. In reality, God is the source of all these things.

Instead of hoarding money for yourself, be generous and build God's house. We don't need fancy church buildings, but we need a healthy church body. As you prepare for your day, think of ways you can bless others.

Father God, I am sorry when I have thought only of myself in terms of my earthly possessions. Help me to see beyond my circumstances today, and look toward being able to bless the body of Christ.

Moved to Help

*Help him to defend the poor,
to rescue the children of the needy,
and to crush their oppressors.*
PSALM 72:4 NLT

When your heart is moved because you see people in poverty, or those who have experienced abuse, or simply those being treated as less than others, you are experiencing a small measure of the compassion that God has for the oppressed. God cares immensely for the suffering that happens in this world, and one day he will restore everything and more to those who have suffered and experienced shame.

Today, if you see or experience some form of oppression, be someone who stands against it. Allow God's compassion in you to reach out to the outcast.

Jesus, I care deeply about people who have experienced being an outcast for any reason. Give me a chance to show compassion and considerate love to someone today.

Freed from Fears

I sought the Lord, and he answered me;
he delivered me from all my fears.
PSALM 34:4 NIV

Fear can be a crippling experience and seems to present itself in all kinds of different scenarios, from physical heights, work presentations, or an upcoming exam to waiting on news from the doctor. When we are full of fear, our bodies prepare us for flight or fight mode, but if neither of those kick in, the feeling of weakness or becoming faint is the next response.

Fear of enemies would have been a very real experience for the Israelites, and it would have meant such freedom for them to know that they would never again have to experience this fear of evil. The same promise can be for you today. God is in your midst and he says, "Fear not!"

Lord, I bring my fears and anxieties to the foot of the cross, knowing that you have given me freedom from these troubles. Thank you that one day all evil will be gone and I will have nothing to fear.

Christ Revealed

The LORD has announced his victory
and has revealed his righteousness
to every nation!
PSALM 98:2 NLT

The day before any big event can be almost exciting as the event itself! We love the anticipation of the good things to come—the day off, the presents, the delicious meal, the gathering of family and friends.

The nation of Israel had a growing expectation that their king was coming, and when news of the birth of Christ finally came to the shepherds, it would have been a glorious day to celebrate. His birth was announced through a great host of angels and it meant salvation for this world. What an amazing event to be a part of. Enjoy the expectancy of tomorrow, today!

Heavenly Father, thank you so much for sending your Son into the world. Thank you that Jesus became human so I could understand that death was defeated and eternal life is freely mine.

Joy to the World

Let the sea and everything in it shout his praise!
Let the earth and all living things join in.
Psalm 98:7 nlt

Joy to the world, the Lord has come! When Christ came as a little child, he not only brought joy to the people of the day that knew he was the Savior, he also brought joy to the entire world.

We celebrate because we know the significance of Christ being born as a human, entering in to our existence, and displaying what it meant to be fully alive. The restoration that Christ brings is something that will extend to all living things, and this is why can have joy on this day—we know that there is hope for the whole created world. Celebrate this hope as you celebrate this day.

Jesus, thank you for showing me what it means to be fully alive. Help me to express joy today as we celebrate your birth.

Stern Warnings

Listen to me, O my people,
while I give you stern warnings.
O Israel, if you would only listen to me!
PSALM 81:8 NLT

It can be hard to hear about the anger or wrath of God when we also know about his unending mercy and unfailing love. We can, however, see God's mercy in the warnings that he sent with the prophets. God cannot tolerate evil; therefore, he gives people a chance to turn away from their sin—this is his mercy.

Ultimately, we know that God provided a way out for the world through Jesus' life, death, and resurrection. God is good and will always provide you with a way out.

Lord, thank you for the day ahead of me. I know that you are not an angry and vengeful God, so I choose to see your warnings as a gracious act for humanity to turn away from wrong. Let me hear your warnings clearly today.

Not Forsaken

Those who know your name trust in you,
for you, O Lord, do not abandon those who search for you.
PSALM 9:10 NLT

God has given us a huge gift in his faithful nature. Unlike our friends, family members, employers, or workmates who will inevitably fail us, God makes promises and sticks to those promises without fail. He can be thoroughly trusted.

How beautiful is this God? He will give you a path to confidently walk on, and he will never abandon you. All you have to do is trust in him.

God, I have been able to reflect on the faithfulness of your character and I am so grateful for it. I have seen the truth of who you are and what you have done for me. Help me to trust in you with everything I have and everything I am.

Unclear Path

In my distress I cried out to the LORD;
yes I prayed to my God for help.
PSALM 18:6 NLT

Can you think of a time where you honestly couldn't see where you were headed? Perhaps that time is now.

Call out to the God who is listening for your voice. He knows where you are. He wants to help you avoid that tangle of roots, or a dangerous drop-off. You will not be unheard. God will answer you, and he will rescue you.

God, I acknowledge that sin has sometimes blinded my path. I have often chosen the way of this world over your ways. Thank you for your forgiveness and ability to cleanse me from all unrighteousness so I can see the way again.

Choosing Praise

I will glory in the Lord; let the afflicted hear and rejoice.
Glorify the Lord with me; let us exalt his name together.
PSALM 34:2-3 NIV

Do we only praise God for something after he has given it, or do we praise him ahead of time in faith, knowing that he will always be good no matter what happens?

We should look at difficulties in life as miracles waiting to happen—chances for God to show his goodness and bring us closer to his heart. Can you let yourself believe this today?

God, at times I admit it is difficult to praise you. Sometimes I don't see you in my life and I don't recognize you in other people's lives either. The news of the day can be depressing. But I choose praise. The world is discouraging but you are not. I want to praise you at all times.

Every Detail

The LORD directs the steps of the godly.
He delights in every detail of their lives.
PSALM 37:23 NLT

Just when we thought we wouldn't worry about asking God for the details, we read that he delights in them. It makes perfect sense when we make the connection that our lives are all about small details and that God wants to dwell in us.

God cares about your details. As you go about your day, with activities that are big or small, invite God into each detail. This is how you let him help guide your steps—one by one.

God, thank you for being part of all the little things in my life. I invite you in to each thing that I do, not expecting you to command my every step, but believing that you delight in the small details.

Praise Party

Praise the LORD!
Praise God in his sanctuary;
praise him in his mighty heaven!
PSALM 150:1 NLT

The end of the year should be a celebration for you, whether it has been a good year or a difficult year. Take some time to reflect on what your hopes were for this year and allow yourself to mourn the things that didn't go as you had hoped. Picture yourself letting go of that disappointment and asking God to heal the grief.

Now turn your thoughts toward all of the wonderful things that you were a part of, or even something that you achieved on your own over the year. Thank God for graciously guiding you through it all. Then celebrate. Celebrate a year that has come to an end and celebrate that tomorrow you will wake to a new hope.

God, I feel blessed when I think about my year and how you have helped me every step of the way. Thank you for the amazing people who encourage me and bring me joy. Thank you for the challenging times because through them I have grown to become more like you.